The Hicksite Separation

The
Hicksite Separation

*A Sociological Analysis of Religious Schism
in Early Nineteenth Century America*

by

ROBERT W. DOHERTY

RUTGERS UNIVERSITY PRESS
New Brunswick   *New Jersey*

Copyright © 1967 by Rutgers, The State University

Library of Congress Catalogue Card Number: 67-13077

Manufactured in the United States of America
by Quinn & Boden, Inc., Rahway, New Jersey

*This book was manufactured with the assistance of a grant from the
Ford Foundation*

Preface

This essay in the sociology of religion does not seek to be a definitive study of early nineteenth century Quakerism or even of the Hicksite schism of 1827. It focuses on relationships between socioeconomic change and Quakerism as a social institution and, in doing so, tends to minimize other aspects of religion and religious behavior. Biased or not, this study seeks to rise above usual denominational studies and narrative synthesis and to address itself to issues and questions which defy analysis through traditional historical methods. In a broad sense, this essay is a result of my belief that use of structural-functional analysis, as defined by contemporary social science, can greatly advance historical understanding and of my commitment to an organic view of man and his relationship to social and cultural environments.

Many persons and organizations have helped me write this book. A grant from the Rutgers University Research Council freed me from teaching. The manuscript was completed with the support of a grant-in-aid from the American Association for State and Local History. Particular thanks are due James N. Rosenau and the Summer Research Committee of Douglass College–Rutgers University, whose assistance al-

lowed four of my students, Catherine Small, Anita Weis-
haupl, Arlene Cella, and Helen Harris, to do much of the
research on which this study is based.

Frederick B. Tolles and Emery Battis each read the manuscript and offered helpful suggestions. Nicholas B. Wainwright steered me clear of numerous stylistic pitfalls. Much
of my own curiosity about history is due to the inspired
teaching of Wallace E. Davies and Richard S. Dunn of the
University of Pennsylvania. My personal and intellectual
debts to my parents are great and I offer a simple thanks.
This book never would have been completed without the
understanding and sympathy of my wife, Marilyn, who
handled more than her share of the details of day-to-day
living and encouraged me to push on—to work a bit harder.

Parts of this book initially appeared as articles in historical
journals. Chapter III was first published in the *American
Quarterly,* Chapter IV in *Pennsylvania History,* Chapter V
in *Quaker History,* and Chapter VI in the *Pennsylvania
Magazine of History and Biography.* They are reprinted here
with the kind permission of editors Hennig Cohen, Russell
Weigley, Frederick B. Tolles, and Nicholas B. Wainwright.

ROBERT W. DOHERTY

Amherst, Massachusetts
September, 1966

Contents

The Hicksite Separation

I. A Functional View of Religion

In April 1827, Philadelphia Yearly Meeting of the Religious Society of Friends split into two new and bitterly antagonistic organizations. The Separation spread and soon involved most Friends in America. This book is an analysis of the social bases for that schism. It argues that controversy over religious belief and practice involves issues seemingly outside the religious sphere and that religion, when studied as a social institution, must be seen in relation to its sociocultural environment.

Historians have studied religion from many different viewpoints. They have examined religion as a belief system, religion as an institution, and religion as an expression of the economic structure of society. They have applied the term religion to such diverse phenomena as Medieval Catholicism, Christian Science, Communism, and Father Divine's Peace Mission. This variety of approach and subject matter is an outgrowth of the complexity of religious behavior and of the different purposes of those who study it. No single approach contains the whole "truth" about religion. The functional view taken in this book is not exclusively valid. It suits the purposes of the author, that is, to test certain sociological theories about religious behavior and to understand the underlying causes of the Hicksite-Orthodox Separation in the Society of Friends.[1]

A functional approach to religion assumes a holistic view of society. Religion is but one part of a social whole in which there is mutual interaction among the parts. In this sense, religion is a set of beliefs and practices through which men seek to adjust themselves to their environment. All religions seem to possess certain universal functions: to explain evil, death, injustice, and suffering. Religion seeks to provide supra-empirical answers to men's ultimate questions. It attempts to allay stresses produced by man's capacity to anticipate the future and imagine ideal states.

> The human individual . . . [possessed] . . . of the power of language, capable, therefore, of anticipating the future, . . . able to verbalize ideal states, to create standards, is continually threatened with failure, with frustration, with his conception of justice unfulfilled. These problems tend to loom up as overwhelming or "absolute evils." Religion is man's attempt to "relativize" them by interpreting them as part of some larger good, some conception of the absolute that puts the individual's problems into new perspectives, thus to remove or reduce their crushing impact. At the same time, man's social relations, his societies, are threatened by these same problems. Fear and hostility can lead to disrupting hostilities, unless they can be reinterpreted as part of a shared experience. In addition to that, there is the tendency of each individual to think only of himself, to make his joys, his desires into "absolute goods," threatening the patterns of mutual adjustment that social life requires. Religion is the attempt to relativize the individual's desires as well as his fears, by subordinating them to a conception of absolute good more in harmony with the shared and often mutually contradictory needs and desires of human groups.[2]

No religion has yet succeeded in fulfilling these individual and social functions; religion is an attempt to fulfill them.

Furthermore, religions attempt to fulfill them in different ways.

Many of the functions of religion are latent (unintended) ones. Often a latent function has more significance for the student of religion than the manifest (intended) one. This is only to say that a participant in a religious ceremony is probably unaware that he is at the same time fostering group cohesion, or integrating his conflicting statuses, or allaying his feeling of guilt. Religious participants can scarcely be expected either to tell or know the "truth" about the "reasons" for their activities or the functions those activities fulfill.

The specific functions of religion will tend to vary in terms of the needs of the participants, the nature of the religion, and the character of the socioeconomic and cultural environment in which religion acts. Acceptance of this axiom forces the student of religion to examine religion in relation to its environment. He must see how religion affects and is affected by the "external" world. Because it often presents empirically unmanageable problems, such an approach may well be an unattainable ideal. Therefore, it is sometimes feasible to look only at parts of the whole. The whole must, nevertheless, be kept in mind.

Concepts drawn from the sociology of religion help mitigate some of the problems inherent in a functional approach. Especially useful is the typology of religious groups initially suggested by Ernst Troeltsch in his *Social Teaching of the Christian Churches*. Troeltsch defines two general types of religious groups: the sect and the church. He sees the church as a mature religious group which is highly organized, formal in worship, and territorial in scope. The church functions in the world. It seeks to dominate the world and is thus highly involved in secular affairs.[3]

The sect stands at the opposite extreme. Typically it is in the early stages of development. It is a small exclusive group which draws its members only from among convinced believers. It is loosely organized and relies on spontaneous participation. It rejects prevailing culture standards and seeks to emphasize a sharp distinction between its members and the world. It is likely to place strong emphasis upon works.

Sect and church are best seen as poles between which a variety of religious forms exist. In fact, no actual religion conforms to these two ideal types. It is important to note the different emphases and thus the different appeals which sects, churches, and their variants may possess.

The historian must adapt these concepts drawn from the sociology of religion to his own purposes. His primary concern is, of course, the relationship between religion and change. A functional approach suggests the basis for understanding this relationship. Religion is neither prime mover nor a mere reflection but is, to quote J. Milton Yinger, "one of several 'levels of causation,' a force that once set in motion is part of a complex of causes that mutually condition one another." [4] Clearly the influence of religion will vary according to its own character and the circumstances in which it is acting.

For purposes of analysis, it is useful to focus directly on relationships between religion and change and to suggest three hypothetical alternatives: 1) religion may act as a barrier to socioeconomic change; 2) religion may act as a cause of change; and 3) religious change may be the result of socioeconomic change. The alternatives are not mutually exclusive. In any given situation two, even three, of them may be taking place simultaneously.

Because its beliefs and values are imbued with sacredness, religion is highly resistant to change. Religious institutions generally claim divine sanction for their practices and thus efforts to change them may be interpreted as acts against the will of God. Of themselves, human values are highly resistant to change but, when those values are given an aura of sacred-

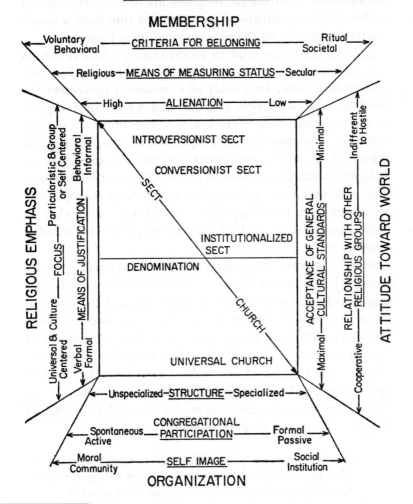

SECT-CHURCH CHARACTERISTICS

MEMBERSHIP

Voluntary / Behavioral ←——— CRITERIA FOR BELONGING ———→ Ritual / Societal

← Religious — MEANS OF MEASURING STATUS — Secular →

← High ——— ALIENATION ——— Low →

INTROVERSIONIST SECT

CONVERSIONIST SECT

SECT

INSTITUTIONALIZED SECT

DENOMINATION

CHURCH

UNIVERSAL CHURCH

← Unspecialized — STRUCTURE — Specialized →

RELIGIOUS EMPHASIS

Particularistic & Group or Self Centered

Universal & Culture Centered

FOCUS

Behavioral Informal

Verbal Formal

MEANS OF JUSTIFICATION

Minimal

Maximal

ACCEPTANCE OF GENERAL CULTURAL STANDARDS

Indifferent to Hostile

Cooperative

RELATIONSHIP WITH OTHER RELIGIOUS GROUPS

ATTITUDE TOWARD WORLD

CONGREGATIONAL PARTICIPATION

Spontaneous Active ←—— ——→ Formal Passive

Moral Community ←— SELF IMAGE —→ Social Institution

ORGANIZATION

ness, they will be very difficult to alter. Whenever religious
beliefs run counter to secular change, they are likely to be
slow to adapt and thus will tend to preserve the status quo.
Furthermore, church-type religions are usually entrenched
in the existing institutional structure and thus have a vested
interest in preserving the structure and their place in it.

Religion may also tend to retard change when it directs
attention away from secular matters toward unachievable
otherworldly aims. In a study of Communist movements in
Sweden, Sven Rydenfelt suggests that Communist organizations compete with sectarian religious groups for their
members. The same kind of people join the two movements.
Wherever one of the movements is strong, the other is weak.
Religious sectarianism thus syphons off potential members
from a secular protest movement and focuses its members'
attentions upon nonsecular goals. In this case, secetarian religion would seem to be inadvertently supporting the existing
situation.[5]

In most cases religion retards, resists, and slows down processes of change, but it also acts as cause and director of these
same processes. Gerhard Lenski in his book, *The Religious
Factor,* builds a strong case for religion as a causal influence.
One of Lenski's purposes was to test Max Weber's contention
that, in so far as religions develop their own distinctive orien-
tations toward major phases of human society, they will in
turn influence the development of other institutions in society. After detailed examination of socioreligious groups in
Detroit, Michigan, Lenski concludes:

> our study has provided striking support for Weber's basic
> assumption—at least as far as it applies to the major re-
> ligious groups in contemporary American society.[6]

Lenski's purposes are essentially those of a sociologist; therefore he does not directly address the historical problem of

change through time. His findings do, however, suggest ways in which religion affects processes of change. He points out that the socioreligious group to which an individual belongs will affect the probability that he will "enjoy his occupation, indulge in installment buying, save to achieve his objectives in the future, believe in the American Dream, vote Republican, favor the welfare state, [oppose] . . . freedom of speech and racial integration," and so on. This statement would seem to be valid for other periods in American history. Lee Benson's study of political behavior in the Jacksonian era comes to similar conclusions.[7]

In periods of sociocultural drift, tendencies such as those noted by Lenski are likely to act as selective agents. That is to say, when change is the result of human interaction which is directed toward ends other than change itself, religious value systems can influence the form and content of the interaction and thus the change which results. Put more simply, the ways in which people respond to things are primary determinants of the direction of change and the nature of the response is likely to be at least partially determined by socioreligious membership.[8]

Religion becomes a more dramatic (but not necessarily more influential) agent of change when it is organized into a goal-seeking movement. Analysis of the influence of such movements is difficult. It demands penetrating study of both the internal characteristics of the movement and relationships between those characteristics and the external world. Goals of the movement must be carefully examined in terms of their avowed objectives and any latent functions which they might have. The quality of goals must also be determined. To what extent do goals depart from existing practice? What is the relationship between goals and prevailing culture standards? Are goals general or specific? When and where are they to be achieved?

Usually goals will be accompanied by a more elaborate belief system or ideology which defines the movement's culture more clearly than do the goals. This ideology seeks to justify the movement, explain its values and ideals, and present rules of behavior. The ideology expands the goals into a base "from which the movement derives its rationale, its doctrine, its course, and its disciplinary principles." [9]

A religious movement must also possess some form of organization. How is it organized? To what extent is the organization structured? Are there established patterns of procedure, rank, and function? Are diverse elements well co-ordinated? What is the character of the leaders? To whom would they appeal or not appeal? How are members admitted? What is expected of them? Does the movement develop a we-they sense of loyalty?

Finally, it is important to note the tactics the movement employs to seek its goals. Are tactics consistent with goals? with culture standards? To whom would tactics appeal? To whom would tactics be distasteful? Are tactics successful in emphasizing the needs and frustrations of actual and potential members?

Once goals and belief system, structure and tactics have been identified, analysis of membership can be undertaken. Two means of classification of members are useful: 1) the relationship of a member to the movement's goals; and 2) the extent to which a member is involved in the movement. Most participants in any social movement will be goal-oriented. They will join the movement because they feel (perhaps unconsciously) that the implementation of its goals will somehow benefit them. In addition to the goal-oriented, there are utilitarians who seek immediate benefits from the movement which have no direct relationship with the movement's goals. They may seek to make a profit, redirect the movement to their own purposes, or simply enjoy being in positions of power. Whatever their motive, they have no commitment to the movement's objectives and ideals. There are also altruists who seem to seek no benefit for themselves but whose purposes are defined in terms of their own psychological needs.

The extent of involvement in a movement varies as widely as the relationship of members to goals. Some members will have almost wholly committed themselves to the cause while others operate only on the fringe, ready to shift away from the movement whenever their interests seem to so indicate. Some may take a position for or against the movement only when they are forced to do so. Extent of involvement is best seen as a continuum ranging from intense commitment to neutrality to intense opposition. Clearly then, the members of a social or religious movement do not constitute a homogeneous group.

Implicit in this lack of homogeneity is a difference between leaders and followers. Leaders must be identified and their motives assessed. Other levels of participation and function should also be analyzed. Usually the simple leader-follower dichotomy will prove to be too simple and intermediate functionaries will also be found. Who are they and what are their motives? How do these functionaries or active participants differ from leaders on the one hand and followers on the other?

Possession of all the internal characteristics necessary for success is no guarantee that a religious movement will promote change. A movement often becomes a functioning entity without attaining its ends. On the other hand, a movement may fail internally and yet ultimately achieve its goals. In secular, heterogeneous, industrial societies, a religious movement is probably most influential when acting as a gadfly, but in societies where religion is more pervasive, especially when it is the primary means of interpreting experience, religious movements are more likely to be of direct causal influence.

Religious movements can be more easily understood as religious changes resulting from social change. Religious movements are usually responses to alterations in the environment.

They are likely to occur as a result of cultural confusion, social heterogeneity, and individual discontent.

In any society, at any time, there will be elements of inconsistency and instability, that is, cultural confusion. Expectations of some of the norms of society and its subgroups will be dysfunctional to society as a whole. The goals of a society may be unclear. The accepted means of achieving those goals may not be available to all members of society. Some facets of the means may be contradicted by other social values. Consequences for alternative courses of action may be ambiguous. Old values may not be readily adaptable to new situations. Patterns of prestige and advancement may be deranged.[10]

Societies are most susceptible to cultural confusion in periods of rapid change. Even a society which is highly integrated is likely to be strained by a markedly increased rate of change. Values and patterns of behavior which were once functional tend to lose their meaning and usefulness. Readjustment can be both slow and painful. Indeed, confusion as a result of cultural lag seems to be endemic in modern society.

Cultural confusion is also more likely to occur in heterogeneous societies. When a society is made up of many religious, ethnic, and regional subgroups, when its members pursue a variety of occupations, when its members live in diverse physical and social environments, it is inevitable that opportunities for conflicts of norms and values are increased. This is not to say that such situations do not occur in relatively homogeneous societies, but only to emphasize that the potential is greater in heterogeneous ones.

Cultural confusion and social heterogeneity both contribute to the growth of religious movements, but ultimately it is the response of individuals to these conditions which provides the base from which such movements grow. It is the discontent of individuals which a movement must tap. The sources and forms of discontent are extremely varied. Discontent can be diffuse or specific, intense or weak, goal-directed or amorphous. Despite its variety, a few general sources of discontent are worth noting. Individuals are likely to manifest discontent when they are unable to find a minimal coherence and meaning in their lives; when their status or their attitude toward it is not given support and recognition; when the demands of their various roles are in serious conflict; when their goals or values are threatened; and when they are unable to make progress toward their goals.

Discontented individuals frequently do not understand the "real" reasons for their discontent. They are "often bewildered, confused, knowing something is wrong but not knowing why." They have feelings of uneasiness and apprehension. These feelings grow out of an inability to interpret and understand the problems from which they stem. Some persons successfully cope with this kind of stress through withdrawal; others continue to suffer under tension until they find an explanation which will give meaning to their situation.[11]

Obviously all discontented individuals do not join religious movements. Religion is but one among many means of escaping from or explaining discontent. In order to gain adherents a religious movement must strike precisely the right combination of goals, beliefs, and tactics, and even then many of its potential members will not join or will remain on its fringes. People are likely to be most receptive to such movements when they lack an adequate mental context to explain their discontent or when they have a fixed mental context with which the movement is in direct agreement.[12]

Discontent becomes a more active influence when it is accompanied by a crisis which focuses attention on it. This sort of crisis represents in a single event a long series of dissatisfactions. It cuts through routine responses and urges the individual to seek out new solutions for his dilemmas.[13]

In order to function as an activator, a crisis must have this representative quality. It must somehow symbolize the individual's frustrations. When it does, and when the individual feels that his burdens are unjust and can be eliminated, he will be highly susceptible to the suggestions of a social movement. Crisis is not an inevitable companion of social movements but it certainly contributes to their growth.

The classic cases of religious movements as a result of social change are those which have drawn their members from among the socially disinherited. Perhaps the best known of such movements is the early Christian Church, but numerous other examples come quickly to mind. Jehovah's Witnesses, Holiness sects, Sweet Daddy Grace, and Father Divine's Peace Mission all fit into this category.

The appeal of these movements lies in the assurance of self-respect, security, and purposefulness which they provide for their members. Members may be told that the world is only a testing place and that they will be rewarded in heaven for their trials on earth. Members may also be assured that the affairs of the world are unimportant and that imminent destruction awaits unbelievers or that Christ will soon return to reward true believers. The disinherited are thus convinced that prestige and power in the world are not to be desired and that they are the truly good and holy people rather than those who have achieved secular distinction.

The prevalence of religious movements of the disinherited should not hide the fact that religious movements, even sectarian ones, sometimes draw their members from among upper social levels. Emery Battis points out in his *Saints and Sectaries* that the mystical sectarianism of Anne Hutchinson had strong appeal for well-to-do seventeenth century Boston merchants because her ideas would release them from tensions inherent in the then dominant Puritan ethic. Similarly, the Moral Rearmament Movement of Frank Buchman in the nineteen thirties had strong upper-class appeal. It is important, then, to see religion as a means of allaying discontent at all social levels.[14]

* * *

The present study seeks to apply this general theoretical framework to the Hicksite-Orthodox Separation in the Society of Friends. Further discussion of the evolution of religious sects is taken up in Chapter III in connection with the split among Philadelphia Friends, but that discussion only expands theoretical material presented above. The plan of the remainder of the book is relatively simple: first, to present a narrative description of the events and ideas which provoked the Separation; second, to analyze the characteristics of members of the two groups which resulted from the Separation; and third, to seek to explain factors which caused individuals to join one group or the other. It is my hope that the book will successfully demonstrate the usefulness of a functional approach and will show how sociological theory can aid historians in their efforts to understand the past.[15]

II. The Story

In the months before Philadelphia Yearly Meeting of 1827, Friends were apprehensive. The discord which had troubled the Society for several years had been particularly bitter during the winter of 1826–27 and Yearly Meeting was likely to provoke further controversy. Chances for compromise were small. In fact, the leaders of the two main factions, Hicksite and Orthodox, were more concerned with furthering their own views than they were about preserving Quaker unity.

Yearly Meeting was unusually crowded when it opened on April 16, 1827. The very first session confirmed the suspicions of each faction about the other. Orthodox Friends thought the Hicksites were trying to pack the house, and Hicksites felt that the Orthodox were seeking to postpone important business until the delegates became too tired to engage in debate. An hour-long sermon by a militant Orthodox minister from England made the situation even worse.[1]

John Comly, assistant clerk of the Meeting and a leader of the Hicksites, describes the scene:

> At half-past one the meeting adjourned till four; and I had no doubt this first sitting was protracted with a view to crowd the representatives, so as to prevent their agree-

ment in a change of clerks. The image of jealousy was seen standing in the entry, and it provoked to jealousy. The representatives stayed together, and had a boisterous time. It was not like a calm, deliberative body of brethren, but all was disorder and confusion; and the time for the adjourned sitting of the Yearly Meeting arrived before they had come to an agreement, when a few determined partisans [informed] the Yearly Meeting that the representatives could not agree on the selection of a clerk. All was excitement and confusion, when, the doors being opened, the multitude rushed in and prevented any further discussion or conclusion, or even the adjournment of the representatives, who had thus been closely confined for six hours without any refreshment. Such a melancholy scene was probably never exhibited since Friends were people.[2]

Disorder strengthened Comly's already strong belief that Friends could no longer sit together in peace. Comly was not alone in his convictions. Many others also felt that it would be better to withdraw from the Meeting than to perpetuate discord, and since the Orthodox faction controlled almost all the positions of influence, anti-Orthodox or Hicksite Friends began to look toward organizing a Yearly Meeting of their own.

While Yearly Meeting was still in session, Hicksite Friends held a series of gatherings in another meetinghouse in Philadelphia. These meetings were peaceful and well attended. Comly estimated that 600 persons were present at one gathering. After three days of deliberation the anti-Orthodox group issued an address to the members of Philadelphia Yearly Meeting. The time of issuance coincided with the closing of the regular Yearly Meeting.

The address emphasized the importance of love and unity among Friends and the right of freedom of conscience: [3]

early Friends gave ample proofs of the . . . influence of the "new commandment" which Christ gave to his disciples when he said, "A new commandment I give unto you, that ye love one another. . . ." Through obedience to it, [early Friends] became known and distinguished: acting under its sacred influence . . . they were made powerful instruments in opening the door of gospel liberty. . . . Hence they were prepared to promulgate the glorious truth that *God alone is the sovereign Lord of conscience,* and that with this unalienable right, no power, civil or ecclesiastical, should ever interfere.

Early Friends, said the address, enjoyed freedom of conscience and yet maintained unity because of their commitment to the Light Within. They avoided theological speculation. Now, however, unity was gone.

The unity of this body is interrupted . . . a division exists among us. . . . Doctrines held by one part of society . . . are pronounced by the other part to be unsound and spurious.

Without unity the Society cannot function. Its very purpose is denied. Oppression has become the rule of the day. Under these circumstances,

we feel bound to express to you . . . that the period has fully come in which we ought to look towards making a quiet retreat from this scene of confusion.

Retreat they did. Friends would not sit together in Meeting again for more than a century.

Orthodox Friends denied the validity of the address. They, not the authors of this false document, were the true heirs of the early Friends. The authors of this address and their followers preached infidelity. They were Unitarians, Deists, and freethinkers, not true Friends. The Orthodox felt there could be no unity with such men. Unbelievers must be disowned. Thus the two sides were drawn: Hicksites accused the Orthodox of lack of love and forbearance, of oppressive denial of freedom of conscience, and of theological speculation; while the Orthodox branded Hicksites as believers of false doctrines with whom there could be no unity.

The Separation which began in Philadelphia in the spring of 1827 quickly spread into Indiana, Ohio, Maryland, and New York and inaugurated a period of doctrinal discord which troubled Friends for many years to come. No sooner had Quakers split into Hicksites and Orthodox than schisms began to occur within the two groups. Gurneyite, Wilburite and Progressive factions all emerged before the Civil War. Once begun, schism was hard to stop.

From an organizational viewpoint the Hicksite Separation seems to present a tragic and irrevocable means of resolving tensions which had troubled Friends since the seventeenth century: schism, not compromise, was now the way to settle differences among Friends. Yet despite the tragedy, despite all the bitter controversy, there were compensations. The series of splits that took place during the second quarter of the nineteenth century ushered in a period of dynamic activity among Friends. Never had Quakers been more active in so many worthwhile causes. Doctrinal antagonism and religious enthusiasm apparently stimulated Friends toward action, toward service to their fellow men. The truly tragic period came later when both enthusiasm and activity declined.

* * *

The history of the Society of Friends in America (–1827) falls largely within what one historian of Quakerism has termed an Age of Quietism. By 1700 the volatile universal faith preached by George Fox and other early Quakers had subsided. Friends gave up their desire to convert the world to Quaker truths and sought to preserve those truths for themselves. An exclusiveness grew among them. They began to define themselves as a distinct community which must preserve itself in the face of a hostile world.

Except for the decline of universalism, Friends in America retained the essential qualities of seventeenth century Quakerism. They continued to emphasize that the spirit of God lay within all men. They felt that this spirit or Inner Light was the primary basis for religious authority. Neither an infallible church nor the outward revelations of the Scriptures alone could lead man to divine truth. God was still present in the universe and He continuously revealed Himself to man through the Light Within.[4]

Quakerism was a kind of prophetic religion. It avoided outer forms and relied upon a direct apprehension of God. Friends required no intermediary whether church or priest or Bible. Their search for God depended upon an inward immediate experience of His presence.

Pushed to the extreme, this doctrine of the Inner Light seems to point toward spiritual anarchy. However, this was not the case. Friends practiced a form of group mysticism. Gathered together in silence, Friends felt the presence of God to be more immediate than when they worshiped alone. Since God and the Light were one, then true revelations must also be one even though they might not at first appear to be so. The practice of group worship and the strong sense of community among Friends reflected their faith in the unity of man and man, and man and God.

During the eighteenth century, Friends worshiped according to the tenets of quietism. They believed that in order for Divine Will to enter into the soul man must first suppress self-centered human impulses. The activities of the creature—pride, lust, greed—must give way. The search for God begins with the surrender of all willful human desire. The quietist sits silently, free from creature needs, expectantly awaiting God to fill his being with Divine Spirit.

Quietism did not necessarily produce quiet people. The search for God employed negative techniques but the eventual results were often quite positive. Quietism allowed its adherents to strip themselves of convention and measure things against universal truth. Quietism could and often did lead to social reform. The well known Quaker humanitarian, John Woolman, was a quietist, yet he pioneered in many areas of social reform, most notably in the abolition of slavery.

A strong strain of perfectionism ran through this mystical-quietist impulse. Friends envisioned the possibility of a truly moral society in which the spirit of God would reign supreme among men. Short of perfection, men should live according to the Quaker faith in peace, equality, and simplicity. Friends felt war and violence to be contrary to the dictates of Christian love. They refused to support or participate in military ventures and other forms of physical violence. Friends felt that, since all men possessed the spirit of God within them, all men must be equal in His eyes. Thus, they recognized no graduations of social rank or wealth nor did they accept the superiority of one sex to the other. Friends were also convinced that men should live unostentatious lives. They should shed superfluities—music, fancy clothes, the theater—for a moral life of simplicity.

Eighteenth and early nineteenth century Quakerism might well be described as a perfectionist religion dedicated to the ideals of peace, equality, and simplicity. It took the form of group mysticism and was committed to the tenets of quietism. Quakerism was not so much a set of doctrines as it was an inner experience which led to a way of life.

*   *   *

To some extent, crises like the one which occurred in 1827 were an inevitable outgrowth of the character of the Society of Friends. Both Quaker belief and organization helped provoke attitudes and opinions which caused recurrent periods of crisis.

The Society lacked any institutional means for resolving conflict. Quaker organization was primarily based on precedent and had the amorphous quality of something which had been developed slowly through practice. Since the Society was not tightly organized, precise relationships among different bodies were not defined. Thus, for example, methods of appointment and problems of jurisdiction could easily become the subject of controversy. More important, all decisions were supposed to be unanimous. Rather than put issues to a vote, Quakers sought to obtain unanimous approval for decisions which they made. Even though this system of unanimity was not always followed, Friends had no means of resolving serious points of difference. If the Quaker spirit of unity, tolerance, and brotherhood gave way as it did in 1827, there was no institutional recourse.

Quaker beliefs were also a source of difficulty. The commitment of Friends to the ideals of peace, equality, and simplicity meant that Friends could not fully participate in the affairs of the world. As Friends became affluent and gained influence and prestige in secular affairs it became increasingly difficult for them to uphold the Society's restrictions against worldly activities.

In many ways the history of the post-seventeenth century Friends can be written in terms of this struggle between Quaker ideals and worldly practice. For example, in the middle of the eighteenth century, Friends dominated the colony of Pennsylvania. At that time, western Pennsylvania was a center of armed conflict between England and France. If Friends were going to continue to control Pennsylvania politics it became increasingly apparent that they would in some way have to support the war. Friends were faced with a difficult choice between peace principles and political power. If they gave up political control it would mean the end of the "Holy Experiment," for Pennsylvania would come into the hands of the world's people. If they retained control it would necessitate serious compromise with the world. Friends chose to uphold their peace principles and withdrew from politics. Other Quaker principles could, and did, create tensions and dilemmas similar to those of the mid-eighteenth century war crisis.[5]

If, on the one hand, the Separation of 1827 was due to certain universal tendencies within the Society, it can also be attributed to the unusual environment in which it took place. Processes of social, economic, and intellectual change were so disruptive that they placed severe strain on all religious organizations, not just the Quakers. Methodist, Congregationalist, Presbyterian, and Baptist churches also split during the first half of the nineteenth century.

Early nineteenth century America was on the eve of an industrial revolution. Transportation was improved through the building of turnpikes, canals, and railroads. New forms of economic organization were tried and new techniques of production employed. Specialization took place in many types of economic enterprise. Economic relationships became more impersonal. American manufacturing grew. Commercial agriculture increased. In short, the basic structure of American social and economic relations was being changed.

These changes affected all Americans. However, their impact was greatest in the Eastern and Middle Atlantic states and was especially strong in areas near large seaboard cities like Philadelphia. The process taking place was a new one for Americans. The eighteenth century had been relatively stable. Patterns of prestige and advancement were widely understood and generally accepted. To be sure, there was change in the eighteenth century, but it was change which still tended to leave things pretty much as they had been before. By 1820, this was no longer so. Change began to eat away at the foundations of eighteenth century stability. The nineteenth century was to be an age of disorder.

Americans in 1815 were scarcely aware that historians would one day look back upon that date as a "watershed" in the nation's history. Certainly they had no great understanding of the changes taking place around them, yet they were forced to respond to an altered environment. Some found new opportunities. Some saw opportunities but felt they were denied access to them. Others saw no opportunities but rather felt their positions in society weakened. They looked with nostalgia to a bygone world which was more congenial to them.

The process of socioeconomic change was unsettling in its own right but it was accompanied by equally disturbing alterations in the religious and political climate. By 1830 America was deeply involved in a populist-democratic political experiment. The period 1808–1844 was one of fundamental political realignment. New issues came to the fore. New political techniques were employed. The common man and his search for equality of opportunity became a, perhaps the, central theme of political debate. Egalitarian sentiment pervaded all levels of politics and society. It was not the special ideology of any one party or social class. Since its emphasis was more on opening up opportunity and removing special privilege than it was on simple equality, egalitarianism did not lead to a class-conscious struggle between rich and poor, but it did act as a wedge between social classes and made men more aware of their position in society.

A wave of religious enthusiasm also swept across early nineteenth century America. Revival after revival stirred the souls and emotions of the "sinful multitude." Bible and tract societies were formed. The Sunday school movement got under way. Missionary activity flourished. People debated the use of Sunday mails. Some ministers even spoke of the need to create a Christian political party. In the midst of this fervor, doctrinal issues were widely debated, and while religious orthodoxy dominated the situation, many opinions were voiced and in some cases nonorthodox views met with considerable success. It was a period which contained such diverse impulses as the free thought experiments of Robert Dale Owen and Francis Wright and the millenarianism of William Miller and the Millerites. Variety and enthusiasm best describe the religious scene.

* * *

Even though the environment was conducive to religious controversy and even though the Friends had certain internal weaknesses which pushed them toward schism, it is important to look briefly at the specific precipitants of the Hicksite-Orthodox Separation. Universal tendencies may well explain the potential for separation but they will not explain why such a separation actually took place. It is the series of specific incidents occurring between 1819 and 1827 which caused these universal tendencies to erupt into an open break.

Much of the controversy which eventually provoked the Separation centered on the ideas of Elias Hicks (1748–1830). Hicks was a Quaker minister from Long Island. As a youth he had tried his hand at many trades—carpentry, teaching, and surveying—but had finally turned to farming, an occupation which he found noble and rewarding.

Hicks loved the countryside. To him, nature was a gift which God had placed before man for his enjoyment. However, it was not God's plan that man should sit idly contemplating the beauties of the land. Man must labor. Through work he immerses himself in God. Hicks enjoyed working in the fields. He commented in his *Journal:* [6]

> Laboured hard in my harvest field. . . . I found I could wield the scythe nearly as in the days of my youth. It was a day of thankful and delightful contemplation. My heart

was filled with . . . gratitude to [God for] . . . care over me, in preserving me in health, and in possession of my bodily powers, the exercise of which were still affording me both profit and delight; and I was doubly thankful for the continued exercise of my mental faculties [for they aid me] in contemplating the works of nature and Providence, in the blessings and beauties of the field.

Hicks was moved early in his life to take up the ministry. As a minister he had remarkable success. Great crowds gathered to hear him and those who heard his message were deeply inspired. Hicks had a gift for speaking. His appearance—"tall straight figure, clean shaven, large clear black eyes, long white hair"—added an additional dimension to his natural eloquence. Hearing Elias Hicks was an experience a man was not likely soon to forget.[7]

Hicks's ideas were basically those of a quietist. He vigorously urged Friends to shun creaturely activity. Man, he thought, needs to turn his attention away from the outer world and center his mind and spirit on the inner world of Christ. Hicks felt that man must rely on his own experience. Once the creature had been subdued, outer revelation, ritual, and doctrine were all irrelevant.

The focal point of Hicks's doctrine was his emphasis on the Inner Light. The Light alone was sufficient for salvation. Nothing outward was necessary. If the Light was allowed to express itself, it would lead man toward God. In his *Journal,* Hicks made his position clear: [8]

My mind was much engaged to turn the attention of the people from man, and from all dependence on anything without them, to the inward principle of divine light and truth . . . The best [that] outward . . . help, either from reading the scriptures, or hearing the gospel preached . . . can do for any man, is to lead the minds of the children of men home to this divine inward principle manifested in their own hearts and minds.

Hicks's rejection of original sin was a natural outgrowth of his emphasis upon the Light Within. Sin was not inherited. Man was born free. Sin lay in the self-will of the creature. A sinful man was one who turned away from the Light and lived in the darkness of his own creaturely desires.

Hicks's ideas were not especially new. Certainly they should not be termed either modern or liberal. He was primarily a prophet of the past. However, his heavy emphasis on the Inner Light did lead him to express some doctrines which departed from usual Quaker belief. He pushed quietism so far that he destroyed the balance among different strains of Quaker thought.

If the Light Within is the unerring guide to God and salvation, the Bible must assume a secondary importance. It is an outward help and should not be idolized. The role of Christ as a mediator is also reduced. Indeed, Hicks totally rejected the idea of mediation. He interpreted Christ as a man who had truly lived within the Light. Like every other man, Christ possessed divinity within him, but He could be interpreted as divine only in the sense that He had absorbed Himself in the Light. Christ could not, then, be an agency for redemption. Salvation demanded a surrender of the will and living in the Light. Understandably, Hicks found the idea of a trinity no more palatable than that of Christ's redemptive powers.

Hicks presented his views with considerable force. He had organized them so clearly and delivered them with so much vigor that they were bound to offend people who disagreed with him. Hicks was inclined to be dogmatic about the validity of his views and was frequently intemperate in his language. For example, he said that people who used goods produced by slaves were no better than thieves and murderers. It is possible that some of Hicks's pugnacious dogmatism was due to his age. He was 72 in 1820. Whatever the source, Hicks's position was not one of breadth, tolerance, and love.

Hicks's social views were also a source of friction. He believed that Friends must live apart from the world. Friends should not become absorbed in secular pursuits nor should they associate with non-Friends. Hicks pushed these basic views to extreme conclusions. He urged Friends not to join any organization which contained non-Quakers. He rejected books, science, and public schools as purveyors of the world's wisdom. "Studying to be . . . learned in the sciences . . . ," wrote Hicks, was "as trivial as . . . ribbons on [a] young woman's head." To Hicks, a good Friend was one who worked hard, lived simply, rejected the world, and sought God.[9]

A strong anti-modern strain runs through the ideas of Elias Hicks. He disapproved of man-made improvements like the Erie Canal. He is reputed to have said, "If the Lord had intended there should be internal waterways, he would have placed them there, and there would have been a river flowing through central New York." Hicks was also a strong opponent of early attempts to build railroads. He seemed to feel that certain tasks were better left in the hands of God.[10]

Hicks's greatest social contribution was his forthright attack on Negro slavery. In 1811, he published a pamphlet arguing against the institution of slavery. Hicks's words were strong. Men who upheld slavery in any way were committing a sin in the eyes of God. Hicks vividly described the horrors of slavery and the slave trade. He urged Friends to abstain from the use of slave products. Later, he became interested in schemes to colonize freedmen.[11]

*   *   *

Hicks's views on slavery were involved in the first of the incidents leading up to the Hicksite-Orthodox Separation. In 1819, he delivered a sermon in the Men's Meeting at Pine Street in Philadelphia. He dwelt heavily upon the growth of a worldly spirit among Friends and roundly criticized Friends who used the products of slave labor. Apparently he also urged young Friends to follow the dictates of their conscience even if this caused them to disobey their elders. Hicks stressed the overriding importance of behavior as a measure of a man's religion.

Neither Hicks's ideas nor the directness of his presentation were calculated to comfort his audience. In fact, several of his listeners were very much disturbed. Hicks's statements were interpreted as a challenge by the leaders of the Philadelphia Quakers. They felt that his accusations were directed at them —that he was calling them unholy and questioning the validity of their leadership. Jonathan Evans, a long-time elder, was particularly offended. At his insistence, the Meeting adjourned while Hicks was still addressing the Women's Meeting. This was an unusual procedure and could only be interpreted as an insult to Hicks. Soon after the close of the Meeting Jonathan Evans spoke with Hicks. Each man felt that right was on his side, and they parted without resolving their differences.

Three years later Hicks was again in the Philadelphia area. Much had changed since 1819. In the intervening period a series of articles defining the Quaker position had appeared in a Wilmington religious magazine. Several influential Philadelphia Friends felt that these articles misinterpreted Quaker belief, and that they presented un-Christian ideas. These same Friends also had come to feel that Hicks himself was guilty of preaching false doctrines.

Hicks's visit in 1822 was bound to stir up controversy. It did. The Philadelphia leaders said that Hicks was unfit for the ministry and made a series of attempts to silence him. For the most part, they concentrated on Hicks's doctrinal views rather than his social ones. The reasons for this emphasis are many. Hicks's peculiar doctrinal opinions certainly lent themselves to this kind of attack. Contemporary religious climate encouraged doctrinal argument and, perhaps most important, the Philadelphia leaders—the Orthodox faction—

did not want to probe deeply into areas where they were particularly sensitive, that is, their relationship with the world.

Hicks never directly responded to Orthodox accusations that he denied the existence of the Trinity, the divinity of Christ, His role in the atonement of man, and the importance of the Bible. He simply rejected the significance of these accusations. His efforts to defend himself were in terms of what he felt were departures from proper procedure on the part of Philadelphia leaders. Hicks's friends, however, took up the charges against him and attempted to refute their validity.

After the confrontations of 1822, the dispute widened. Friends generally knew of the events which had taken place and began to divide into the supporters and opponents of the Philadelphia elders and supporters and opponents of Hicks. During the next five years differences between the two groups increased. Each side suspected the other of plotting against it. Each accused the other of departing from Quaker tradition. Each came firmly to believe in the sole righteousness of its position. Friends were no longer friends. Tempers flared. Shouts of popery, oppression, heresy pierced the silence of First Day morning. Thus the way was prepared for Yearly Meeting in 1827 and the Hicksite-Orthodox Separation.

The antagonisms which provoked the split were actually a good deal more complex than they might at first seem. Beneath the surface, the controversy involved issues which went to the very heart of Quakerism. Specifically, such questions were raised as: who should be a member of the Society of Friends, how should the Society be organized, how does a Friend seek salvation, and to what extent should a Friend accept the ways of the world? More generally, the debate between Hicksite and Orthodox centered on the problem of who is a holy man and how does one recognize him? The answers which the two groups gave to these questions reflect different value systems and different interpretations of the nature of Quakerism.

The Orthodox wanted to make their peace with the secular world. They endorsed a formal religion which would emphasize belief rather than behavior—a system which would allow them to participate in the affairs of the world without the tensions produced by an emphasis on quietism and fulfillment of a behavioral code. They no longer wanted to hamper creaturely activity to the point where human power was humbly limited. In short, they wanted a religion that would give meaning to, that is, sanction and recognize their activities in the world. Thus, they stressed the importance of doctrine. A religious man was, in their eyes, one who believed in a specified set of religious ideas. This emphasis on belief left considerable leeway as to what constituted proper behavior.

The Orthodox also intimated that secular success might well be used as a guide to one's spiritual progress. They argued that the leadership of the Society of Friends should be put in the hands of the well-to-do. Important offices should be filled by these men. They should determine which beliefs were proper and which were not. The general membership should be passive and let the problems of belief, membership, and salvation be resolved by those on whom God had granted His blessing in the form of material wealth. It seems, then, that the Orthodox sought to create a religious situation which would allow them considerable latitude in behavior and would grant them religious recognition for secular success.

Elias Hicks and the general Hicksite impulse opposed these Orthodox objectives. Hicks was an outsider who challenged the leadership of the well-to-do in Philadelphia. He branded them as "unholy men" because they did not live up to specified works. Far from recognizing their secular success, Hicks saw the wealth of the Orthodox leaders as an indication of too much creaturely activity—too much of the world. Few of the other Quakers who eventually became Hicksites fully endorsed Hicks's doctrinal views—the term Hicksite is a misnomer—but they all accepted his general emphases. They endorsed a strong behavioral code. They felt activity not belief was the key to salvation. They refused to accept secular success as a measure of a man's religious influence or to discriminate among their members. They directly opposed the creation of any formal hierarchy and encouraged spontaneous participation of all who felt the spirit of God within them. They restricted creaturely activity and participation in the world. In sum, they endorsed a system of belief and organization which would maintain strong and continuous tension between believer and the world. There was no leeway here. All activity, regardless of its nature, was to be governed by religious standards.

In 1827, Quakerism had thus come to a crisis which threatened its continuance as a religious sect. It is important now to examine in detail the relationship between that crisis and its socioeconomic environment. First, however, it is useful to look at the nature and development of religious sects in general.

III. Sect and Church:
Urban Friends

Time has a peculiarly corrosive effect on religious sects. At their inception, sects offer a nonsecular frame of reference which provides status and security to a membership drawn from among alienated segments of the population. Sects reject the values of the world and substitute their own norms both as a standard of behavior and as a means of seeking salvation. Understandably, new sects also tend to shun formal structuralization for a loose spontaneity relying upon lay participation.[1]

One of the crucial factors in the process of the formation and growth of sects is alienation. Therefore, it is important to define it carefully. Alienation is a form of social discontent. It is a state of mind in which an individual feels that there is a discrepancy between his desires and the realities of his social or personal situation. This attitude may encompass feelings of: 1) inability to influence and/or understand society and one's position in it; 2) estrangement from self and/or social norms; and 3) isolation from society in the form of assigning low values to goals which are highly esteemed by society at large.[2]

Alienation exists within the mind and represents an attitude characterized by tension and estrangement. *It differs*

*from generalized discontent and social anxiety in that it pro-
vokes a rejection of at least some significant portions of prevailing culture standards.*

The strength of a religious sect lies in its ability to give
meaning to the frustrations of alienated individuals. In order
to do this a sect needs to establish a delicate balance among
the world, religious organization and doctrine, and its membership. This is a difficult task. When the character of either
the world or a sect's members change, that sect will become
subject to what might be termed imbalance. Its response to
this imbalance will determine whether or not, and in what
manner it will continue to function; thus, the corrosive effects
of time.

To some extent sects have successfully coped with problems
of imbalance by isolating or insulating themselves from the
world. This does not, however, eliminate problems stemming
from internal change and only delays the effect of external
ones. A sect may postpone resolving imbalance but ultimately
it must come to grips with it or suffer gradual extinction.

The usual response of sects to the tensions of change is to
move in a churchly direction—that is, toward formality, internal specialization, relaxation of their behavioral code, and
increased acceptance of the world. The speed and precise
direction of this process may vary from situation to situation,
but the process itself seems universal.

Typically, the growth of this churchly orientation is the
result of a decline in the general alienation of a sect's members and the emergence of an elite which has achieved success
and status as defined by the outside world. Members of that
elite have a stake in society and are not estranged from the
world. Thus they are caught between their own commitment
to the world and the sect's rejection of it. Since the sect
denies the significance of their achievement and frequently
brands them as "unholy" men, members of the elite are forced
to choose among three alternatives: 1) they may reject the

world and their position in it; 2) they may leave the sect for another religious group which will sanction and recognize the significance of their achievement; or 3) they may seek to re-form the sect according to their own particular needs. The first of these alternatives has never proved very popular.

If the elite chooses to re-form the sect and is successful in its efforts, its success is likely to be accompanied by a schism on the part of those members whose alienation is still high and/or whose needs would not be fulfilled by the program of the elite.

It should be emphasized that the tendency of sects to move in a churchly direction varies with different types of sects and will be rigorously resisted regardless of the kind of sect involved. It must also be pointed out that a church-oriented sect may never come to accept a full church position. It possesses a number of intermediate alternatives.

When viewed from the standpoint of doctrine and organization, the Hicksite Separation seems to follow this pattern of movement from sect to church. Liston Pope, in his *Millhands and Preachers,* lists twenty-one changes which are characteristic of this process. Application of Pope's criteria to Hicksite and Orthodox factions reveals that the Hicksites remained sectarian while the Orthodox had adopted many churchly characteristics.[3] (See pages 36–37.)

The differences between Hicksite and Orthodox belief and organization should be an outgrowth of the divergent religious needs of the members of the two factions. In particular, the Orthodox group, especially its leaders, should evidence a commitment to the world and low alienation and the Hicksites should tend toward high alienation and rejection of the world. The dilemma is how to verify this hypothesis, that is, to measure alienation. Ideally one would like to discover the state of mind of participants in the schism. Particularly important in this respect would be their attitudes toward the world. Unfortunately this can be done only indirectly. Ex-

CHARACTERISTICS OF CHURCH AND SECT

Characteristic Change	HICKSITE			ORTHODOX		
	Sect	Mixed	Church	Sect	Mixed	Church
1. *From* membership composed chiefly of the propertyless *to* membership composed of property owners	x					x
2. *From* economic poverty *to* economic wealth, as disclosed especially in the value of church property and the salary paid to ministers		Does not apply				x
3. *From* the cultural periphery *toward* the cultural center of the community	x					x
4. *From* renunciation of prevailing culture and social organization, or indifference to it, *to* affirmation of prevailing culture and social organization	x					x
5. *From* self-centered (or personal) religion *to* culture-centered religion, from "experience" to a social institution	x					x
6. *From* non-co-operation, or positive ridicule, toward established religious institutions *to* co-operation with the established churches of the community	x					x
7. *From* suspicion of rival sects *to* disdain or pity for all sects		x			x	
8. *From* a moral community excluding unworthy members *to* a social institution embracing all who are socially compatible within it	x					x
9. *From* an unspecialized, unprofessional, part-time ministry *to* a specialized, professional, full-time ministry	x			x		
10. *From* a psychology of persecution *to* a psychology of success and dominance	x					x
11. *From* voluntary, confessional bases of membership *to* ritual or social prerequisites only (such as a certificate	x					x

Scale item	14	4	0	2	6	10
of previous membership in another respected denomination, or training in an educational process established by the denomination itself)	x					x
12. *From* principal concern with adult membership *to* equal concern for children of members		x			x	
13. *From* emphasis on evangelism and conversion *to* emphasis on religious education		x			x	
14. *From* stress on a future in the next world *to* primary interest in a future in this world . . . *from* emphasis on death *to* emphasis on successful earthly life	x					x
15. *From* adherence to strict Biblical standards, such as tithing and nonresistance, *to* acceptance of general cultural standards as a practical definition of religious obligation	x				x	
16. *From* a high degree of congregational participation in the services and administration of the religious group *to* delegation of responsibility to a comparatively small percentage of the membership	x				x	x
17. *From* fervor in worship services *to* restraint; *from* positive action to passive listening	x	x			x	x
18. *From* a comparatively large number of special religious services *to* a program of regular services at stated intervals					x	
19. *From* reliance on spontaneous "leadings of the Spirit" in religious services and administration *to* a fixed order of worship and of administrative procedure	x	x	Does not apply		x	
20. *From* the use of hymns resembling contemporary folk music *to* the use of slower, more stately hymns coming out of more remote liturgical tradition		x			x	
21. *From* emphasis on religion in the home *to* delegation of responsibility for religion to church officials and organizations	x		Does not apply		x	
Total	14	4	0	2	6	10

ORTHODOX LEADERS

Name	Birth-Death	Residence	Occupation	Wealth	Age in 1828
Othniel Alsop	1771–1836	Philadelphia	Vinegar merchant	Estate: $27,000	57
Samuel Bettle	1775–1861	Philadelphia	Clothing merchant	Real estate: $12,000	53
Hinchman Haines	1767–1853	Evesham, N.J.	?	?	61
Jonathan Evans	1759–1839	Philadelphia	Gentleman-lumber merchant	Real estate: $7,500 and wide property holdings in Delaware Co., Pa., estate: $40,000	69
Thomas Stewardson	1762–1841	Philadelphia	Gentleman-merchant	Real estate: $22,500; estate: $70,000	66
Joseph Whitall	1770–1847	Woodbury, N.J.	Lawyer, farmer, teacher	?	58
Thomas Wistar	1764–1851	Philadelphia	Gentleman-merchant	Real estate: $14,700; estate: $81,000	64

ORTHODOX ACTIVE PARTICIPANTS

Name	Birth-Death	Residence	Occupation	Wealth	Age in 1828
Isaiah Bell	1772–1849	Philadelphia	Merchant	?	56
Henry Cope	1791–1865	Philadelphia	Merchant-importer	Estate: $677,000	37
Thomas P. Cope	1767–1854	Philadelphia	Merchant-importer	Estate: $1,500,000	61
Sarah Cresson	1771–1829	Philadelphia	Gentlewoman	Real estate: $13,000	57
Samuel P. Griffiths	1759–1826	Philadelphia	Medical doctor	Real estate: $20,000	deceased
Richard Humphreys	1751–1832	Philadelphia	Gentleman-silversmith	Estate: $91,000	77
William Jackson	1746–1834	Chester Co., Pa.	Gentleman farmer	Described as wealthy; never worked	82
Richard Jordan	1756–1826	Newtown, N.J.	Farmer	?	deceased
Isaac Lloyd	1779–1850	Philadelphia	Merchant	Real estate: $61,000	49
Israel Maule	1779–1828	Philadelphia	Lumber merchant	Estate: $40,000	49
Caleb Pierce	1764–1853	Philadelphia	Hardware merchant	Real estate: $3,000	65
Edward Randolph	1754–1837	Philadelphia	Gentleman-East India merchant	Described as extremely wealthy	74
Joseph Scattergood	?	Philadelphia	Druggist-chemist-manufacturer	Estate: $155,000	?
Leonard Snowden	1751–1832	Philadelphia N. Liberties	China merchant	Estate: c. $8,000	77
Ellis Yarnall	1757–1847	Philadelphia	Gentleman-merchant	Real estate: $10,500	71

HICKSITE LEADERS

Name	Birth-Death	Residence	Occupation	Wealth	Age in 1828
Clement Biddle	1778–1856	Philadelphia	Sugar refiner; importer	Real estate: $3,400	50
Samuel Comfort	1777–1862	Bucks Co., Pa.	Teacher, farmer	?, owned small farm in Bucks Co., Pa.	51
John Comly	1773–1850	Byberry, Pa.	Teacher, author	Estate: $12,700	55
Benjamin Ferris	1780–1867	Wilmington, Del.	Conveyancer, author, artist, surveyor	Estate: $50,814	48
William Gibbons	1781–1845	Wilmington, Del.	Physician	Estate: $2,900	47
Halliday Jackson	1771–1841	Darby, Pa.	Teacher, farmer	Estate (1831): $6,300	57
Abraham Lower	1776–1841	Philadelphia— N. Liberties	Cabinet maker	Estate: $900	52
Samuel Noble	?	Jenkintown, Pa.	Gentleman farmer and bank president	Described as extremely wealthy	?
William Poole	1764–1829	Wilmington, Del.	Silversmith, milling business	Estate: $950	64
William Wharton	1791–1856	Philadelphia	Gentleman; never worked	Real estate: $2,600	37

HICKSITE ACTIVE PARTICIPANTS

Name	Birth-Death	Residence	Occupation	Wealth	Age in 1828
Wiliam Abbott	1778–1853	Philadelphia	Brewer	Real estate: $4,000	50
Edward Garrigues	1795–1889	Philadelphia	Druggist	Real estate: $6,700	33
Isaac T. Hopper	1771–1852	Philadelphia	Tailor	Real estate: 0	57
John Hunt	1740?–1824	Philadelphia	Accountant	?	deceased
Joshua Lippincott	1776–?	Philadelphia	Auctioneer	Real estate: $2,500	52
John Moore	1778–1836	Philadelphia	Medical doctor	Well-to-do; estate c. $6,000	50
Robert Moore	1764–1844	Philadelphia	Medical doctor	?	64
James Mott	1788–1868	Philadelphia	Commission merchant	Real estate: 0; income in 1828, c. $1,650	40
Joseph Parrish	1780–1840	Philadelphia	Medical doctor	Real estate: $5,700	48
Josiah Roberts	?	Philadelphia	Bank teller	?	?
Isaac Townsend	1773–1865	Philadelphia–N. Liberties	Laborer	Estate: $650	55
Joseph Turner	1765–1841	Maryland	Farmer	Wealthy; owned large estate	63
James Walton	1771–1846	Abington, Pa.	Farmer	Estate: $4,089	57
John Watson	1774–1864	Bucks Co., Pa.	Farmer, surveyor	?	54

ternal evidence such as occupation, wealth, and place of residence, must be used to verify an internal state of mind. The dangers inherent in this indirect method are obvious. However, if enough data are collected and if they all point in the same direction, generalization can be relatively accurate. Therefore, the approach used here is quantitative.

It is useful to look first at the leaders and active participants in the Hicksite-Orthodox Separation.[4]

Certainly, in the case of the Orthodox, the data confirm the hypothesis. The active Orthodox possessed wealth and engaged in what would be generally accepted as high prestige occupations. In addition, none of their occupations was particularly threatened by economic change. Orthodox leaders had achieved security, prestige, and material success in the outside world. It is natural that they might want a religious sanction and recognition for their secular success, which would relax the tension between themselves and the world. In principle at least, the Society of Friends was ambivalent about sanction and directly opposed to recognition. Thus, the Orthodox sought to obtain explicit acceptance by modifying Quaker doctrine and organization in a churchly direction.

The Hicksite case is more complex. In theory the Hicksites should evidence a high degree of estrangement, yet the data reveal no consistent socioeconomic characteristics. This absence of pattern stems from the complex nature of Hicksite alienation. It would seem that the alienation of many of the Hicksite leaders was not directly attributable to socioeconomic factors. Nevertheless it is interesting that two of the active Hicksites were skilled artisans and two were laborers in an age which witnessed the decline in the status of people who performed physical labor and, at the same time saw the development of economic specialization under the merchant capitalist. The alienation of these four men might be attributed to their anxieties about social and economic change. Such a conclusion is at best highly tenuous and certainly does not provide any overall insight into the character of Hicksite leadership.

In general, other bases for the estrangement of the Hicksite leaders must be found. This problem is taken up in detail in Chapter VI. Perhaps the following sources of alienation ought to be suggested here: 1) suspicion of the city; 2) commitment to social values which were threatened by Orthodoxy; 3) resentment of Orthodox social climbing; 4) psychological shock resulting from worldly failure; 5) commitment to egalitarianism and/or religious freedom, both of which were felt to be challenged by Orthodoxy.[5]

* * *

An examination of the leaders and active participants does, then, at least partially sustain the sect-church hypothesis. Further support can be obtained from an analysis of the general membership in Philadelphia. Here again, Orthodox alienation should be low and Hicksite high. A crude and not altogether accurate way of measuring alienation is simply to compare the relative wealth of the two groups.[6]

WEALTH OF HICKSITE AND ORTHODOX FRIENDS

WEALTH (real estate in $)	HICKSITE		ORTHODOX	
	Number	Per cent	Number	Per cent
0	19	33	20	22
1–999	11	19	6	7
1000–2999	8	13	23	26
3000–4999	10	17	11	12
5000–6999	5	9	12	13
7000–	5	9	18	20
Total	58	100	90	100

The table clearly suggests that Orthodox Friends were wealthier than Hicksites. A higher percentage of the Orthodox owned real estate and what they owned was more valuable than that of their Hicksite counterparts. This rough comparison can be further refined by concentrating on wealth as a factor in the tendency to become Hicksite or Orthodox.[8]

The diagram further substantiates the relationship of wealth to the Separation. For the most part, wealthy persons became Orthodox while the less well-to-do joined the Hicksites. Even admitting the weakness of wealth as a measure of alienation, the tendency of the data to confirm the hypothesis is so strong that it does seem justifiable to assume that low

WEALTH AS A FACTOR IN THE HICKSITE-ORTHODOX SEPARATION

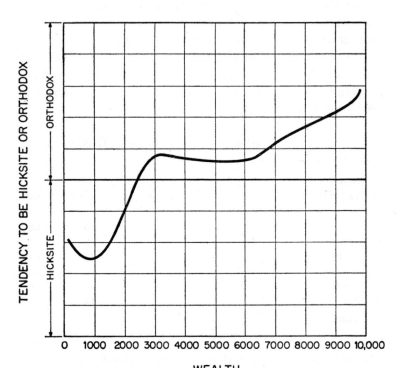

WEALTH
Real Estate in Dollars

and high alienation were characteristic of the general membership of the Orthodox and Hicksite groups.

Further study reinforces this conclusion. Using residence as a measure of social status, it appears that Orthodox Friends tended to live in more expensive neighborhoods and thus, as a group, probably either possessed or aspired to higher social status.[9]

STATUS AND RESIDENCE: HICKSITE AND
ORTHODOX FRIENDS

Electoral Ward	Per Capita Real Estate Assessment	Number of Hicksites	Number of Orthodox
New Market	81	3	3
North Mulberry	121	4	2
Cedar	188	1	3
South Mulberry	189	6	8
Upper Delaware	208	15	7
Lower Delaware	212	17	22
Pine	213	7	9
Locust	217	1	9
North	274	12	26
Dock	328	4	13
Middle	343	5	1
South	385	3	4
Walnut	587	4	11
High	598	16	43
Chestnut	670	5	8
Total		103	169

Another means of measuring alienation is occupation. Orthodox Friends should belong to high status occupations which were not threatened by contemporary economic change and, again, Hicksites should tend toward the opposite extreme.[10]

RESIDENCE AS A FACTOR IN THE HICKSITE-ORTHODOX SEPARATION

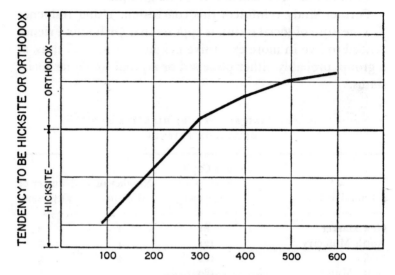

ZONAL REAL ESTATE
Assessment – Dollars per Capita

OCCUPATION DISTRIBUTION OF HICKSITE AND ORTHODOX
FRIENDS IN PHILADELPHIA IN 1828 [11]

Occupation	HICKSITE		ORTHODOX	
	Number	Per cent	Number	Per cent
Gentleman	14	8	34	16
Merchant-Importer	12	7	35	16
Professional	10	6	13	6
Business	45	26	62	29
Semi-Professional	18	11	20	9
Artisan-Labor	71	42	51	24
Total	170	100	215	100

The general tendency of the data is as it should be—the
Orthodox were more inclined to be engaged in occupations
which would bring them both status and wealth. This tend-

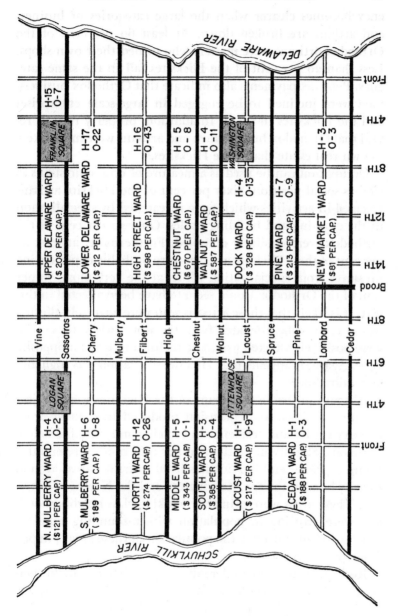

ency becomes clearer when the large categories of business
and artisan are broken down. At least 60 per cent of the
Orthodox artisans were masters who owned their own shops.
Less than 20 per cent of the Hicksites fall in the same category. Poor tax payments also indicate that Orthodox businessmen were inclined to be engaged in large-scale enterprises
and the Hicksites in small. In addition, property records reveal that Orthodox businessmen and artisans were more likely
to own real estate than were Hicksites.[12]

Occupation can be used as a measure of economic status as
well as social position. Sixty per cent of the Hicksite artisans
engaged in activities which were threatened by specialization
in the clothing and building trades. Only 30 per cent of the
Orthodox were similarly occupied. Furthermore, at least 90
per cent of these Hicksite artisans were probably experiencing
pressures from specialization while, at the very most, 70 per
cent of the Orthodox would seem to have been affected in this
way. It is likely that those artisans who were adversely affected
would tend to be alienated from the world while those who
were positively affected would be inclined to take an opposite
view. Again, it appears that Hicksite alienation was high and
Orthodox low.[13]

It is also probable that many of the Hicksites were subject
to cultural shock and confusion produced by a move from
country to city and residence in growing and unstable neighborhoods. Slightly more than 50 per cent of a representative
group of Philadelphia Hicksites lived in fringe areas around
the city like Southwark, Kensington, and the Northern Liber-
ties. These areas were primarily working class neighborhoods
and were growing in population with astounding rapidity.
Between 1820 and 1840, the population in these areas jumped
from 45,000 to 200,000.

Residence in areas undergoing rapid change can be per-
plexing in its own right but for many of the Hicksites it was
doubly so. They had moved from areas outside Philadelphia

PLACE OF RESIDENCE OF PHILADELPHIA FRIENDS [14]

	HICKSITE		ORTHODOX	
	Number	Per cent	Number	Per cent
Philadelphia	170	47	215	75
Northern Liberties	121	34	29	10
Southwark	67	19	44	15
Total	358	100	288	100

into the city and thus came in contact with the demands of a new and potentially confusing social environment—a circumstance which often produces alienation.

URBAN AND RURAL MIGRATION, 1817–1827 [15]

	HICKSITE		ORTHODOX	
	Number	Per cent	Number	Per cent
Country to city	190	51	126	33
City to country	38	10	19	5
None	145	39	237	62
Total	373	100	382	100

These figures should not be interpreted absolutely. The data are taken from Quaker records of certificates of removal and, since certificates often had to be granted in order for someone to be married, they do not always indicate real moves. Nevertheless the figures do suggest that a large percentage of Hicksite Friends had come to Philadelphia and environs from nonurban areas in the ten years preceding the Separation.

It is, then, quite clear that the general membership of the Hicksite and Orthodox factions possessed a pattern of low and high alienation which sustains the sect-church concept.

Bases for alienation or lack of it may vary between leaders, active participants, and general membership but the direction does not. The Hicksite-Orthodox schism was clearly conditioned by socioeconomic pressures on the members of the Society of Friends.

*   *   *

In many ways, the analysis of the Hicksite-Orthodox schism presented here is excessively simple. It seems to suggest that the participants in the schism were consciously seeking to use religion for secular purposes. Nothing could be further from the truth. Both Hicksite and Orthodox Quakers were sincerely engaged in a religious controversy. Nevertheless, religion played such an important role in their lives that any dispute over religion was bound to involve problems of secular behavior.

The Quakers saw their world in religious terms. They did not recognize a dichotomy between religious and secular life. Their world was an organic whole. They interpreted that world through religion. Clearly, though, the religious positions taken by participants in the Separation were in part the result of secular pressures. Considering the organic view of the Friends, this was to be expected.

IV. Sect and Church: Nonurban Friends

Within the city of Philadelphia, the sect-church concept seems to be a useful tool of analysis. It remains to be seen whether it can be extended to areas outside the city. If the sect-church concept is valid for nonurban Quakers, then Hicksite and Orthodox Friends in areas outside Philadelphia should generally evidence the same values and degrees of alienation as did their urban counterparts.

Friends outside Philadelphia were aware of tension within the Society several years before the Separation took place. As early as 1822 the question "is thee a Hicksite or anti-Hicksite?" was being discussed. Nevertheless, no clear lines of division appeared until after Philadelphia Yearly Meeting split in April of 1827. Even then, some Meetings remained together until the spring of 1828.[1]

Initiative for the nonurban Separations came from Philadelphia. Orthodox leaders visited Meetings outside the city. Samuel Bettle, Jonathan Evans, Thomas Stewardson and others traveled through the countryside. Hicksite leaders also took to the road. These visits tended to polarize opinion, especially when leaders were outspoken. The Orthodox cause was certainly damaged by the belligerence of the English ministers who traveled with them. Despite this polarization, the most common issue that provoked outright division was whether to recognize the Hicksite or Orthodox Yearly Meeting.[2]

Approximately 75 per cent of the Friends outside the city joined the Hicksites, but the percentage varied from place to place. In some areas, Orthodox Friends were in a majority. Nevertheless, these variations do follow a pattern. The over-all characteristics of the nonurban Separation were universal enough to justify testing the sect-church concept through a detailed study of one area. Chester and Delaware counties in southeastern Pennsylvania are well suited to this purpose. There were many Quakers in this area. The two counties were highly diversified and thus contained most of the en-vironmental conditions which confronted Friends in the early nineteenth century.[3]

Chester and Delaware counties were among the areas settled by seventeenth century Friends. By the early seventeen hun-dreds the area was scattered with well established farms and had become the center of an antiproprietary faction in the colonial assembly. A coalition of Chester county farmers and Philadelphia artisans managed to survive well into the eighteenth century and continuously opposed the Penn fam-ily and its well-to-do supporters in the city. This so-called "country party" alertly resisted any aristocratic pretensions of the urban rich. Although the country party did not sur-vive the crisis of the American Revolution, it is highly prob-able that some of its traditions did. In any case, Chester and Delaware counties had long been a center of opposition to Philadelphia.[4]

In the early nineteenth century the two counties were still primarily agricultural but they had begun to diversify. Some farmers were employed in domestic industry as well as agri-culture. The numerous creeks in the area were dotted with mills. Each county had its own small villages. West Chester, in Chester county, had, for example, a population of 1,250

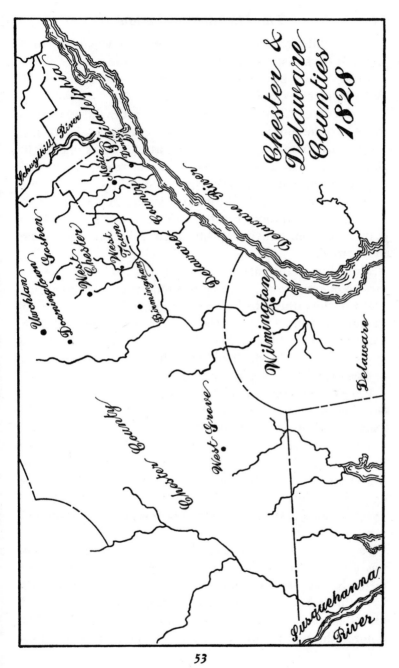

Chester & Delaware Counties 1828

in 1830 and also had a public library, newspaper, bank, farmer's market, school, and fire company. Southeastern Pennsylvania cannot be simply termed rural nor should its residents be merely classified as farmers.[5]

Residents of Chester and Delaware counties did not necessarily lead the simple, isolated lives sometimes associated with a rural environment. They were not as isolated as one might think. They had good transportation via roads, rivers, and stage coaches. They had newspapers and a slow but adequate postal service. Residents of the two counties were cut off from regular and continuous contact with the outside world—they may have been provincial—but their isolation was by no means total.

More important than the lack of total isolation was the growth of commercial farming in southeastern Pennsylvania. Many of the farmers had given up yeoman independence for the lure of profit. They sold their butter, eggs, cheese, poultry, fruit, and vegetables in Philadelphia. Frequently they also fattened beef cattle which had been driven from the mid-west and were awaiting sale in the city.[6]

Profits from commercial farming could be large. Samuel Bunting, a Quaker farmer in Delaware County, began in 1805 with an eight-and-a-half-acre plot and through hard work rapidly expanded his holding. Bunting sold his produce in Philadelphia. He got up regularly at two o'clock in the morning in order to get his goods into the city when the market opened. He invested his profits in land and fruit trees. By 1825 he had a flourishing orchard of several (five?) thousand trees and owned 140 acres of land.[7]

Farming in general, and particularly commercial farming, was given great impetus by the introduction of scientific methods. Between 1800 and 1830, southeastern Pennsylvania went through an agricultural revolution. Long and wasteful use of the soil had exhausted it, but now its fertility was restored through the use of fertilizers and crop rotation. Production per acre was further expanded by the use of labor-saving mechanical improvements.[8]

Agriculture was generally prosperous during the first third of the nineteenth century, but it was subject to insecurities. In addition to ever-present natural hazards, farmers had to cope with the newness of their situation. Change was rapid. Particularly important was the uprooting effect of commercial agriculture. It challenged yeoman ideals. Added to these uncertainties was a sharp drop in the price of land and agricultural goods between 1816 and 1819. Land prices fell from about $200 per acre to $50–80, and agricultural prices fell by one-half and stayed low until after 1830.[9]

Given these conditions, what patterns ought to emerge among Hicksite and Orthodox residents in order to sustain the sect-church concept? If the hypothesis is valid, Orthodox Friends should not be alienated from the world. They should be committed to the values of the acquisitive society around them. They should be benefiting from processes of change. They should be engaged in commercial agriculture and should not have suffered from either the price change of 1816–1819 or the revolution in agricultural techniques. Orthodox Friends might also be expected to dominate non-agricultural occupations. In contrast, Hicksites ought not to be committed to the business values of commercial agriculture. They should be noncommercial farmers who were either not gaining from the new agriculture or were being hurt by it. Their ideals should not be those of the prevailing culture. They should be alienated from the world.

Individual cases suggest that there is some validity in this interpretation. Philip Price, an Orthodox leader from Chester County, used scientific agriculture to great advantage. In 1791 he bought 300 acres of worthless land and through systematic fertilization restored the soil. He sold the land for a sizable profit. Jesse Kersey, a Hicksite leader who was also versed in scientific agriculture, tried to do the same thing. He failed.

Kersey sold his farm at a loss when he could no longer maintain the mortgage payments.[10]

A truer test of the sect-church concept can be obtained by a quantitative comparison of Hicksite and Orthodox Friends. First it is useful to look at the value and size of the farms owned by members of the two factions. While such a comparison is not likely to be profoundly revealing, it should show what kind of individual joined each branch and may suggest areas of contrast between the two groups.[11]

The data suggest that Orthodox Friends owned larger and more valuable farms, but the difference between Hicksite and

VALUE OF FARMS: HICKSITE AND ORTHODOX FRIENDS

Delaware County

VALUE OF FARM (in $)	HICKSITE		ORTHODOX	
	Number	Per cent	Number	Per cent
1–999	9	20	3	9
1000–1999	14	31	8	24
2000–2999	11	24	7	21
3000–3999	4	9	9	27
4000–	7	16	6	18
Totals	45	100	33	99

Chester County

VALUE OF FARM (in $)	HICKSITE		ORTHODOX	
	Number	Per cent	Number	Per cent
0–1999	19	22	12	14
2000–3999	27	31	21	24
4000–5999	16	18	22	26
6000–7999	14	16	11	13
8000–	12	14	20	23
Totals	88	101	86	100

SIZE OF FARMS: HICKSITE AND ORTHODOX FRIENDS

Delaware County

SIZE OF FARM	HICKSITE		ORTHODOX	
(in acres)	Number	Per Cent	Number	Per Cent
1–49	10	23	2	6
50–99	16	37	12	35
100–149	11	26	9	26
150–199	4	9	7	21
200–	2	5	4	12
Totals	43	100	34	100

Chester County

SIZE OF FARM	HICKSITE		ORTHODOX	
(in acres)	Number	Per Cent	Number	Per Cent
1–49	17	20	9	11
50–99	26	30	21	25
100–149	25	29	27	33
150–199	16	18	12	14
200–	3	3	14	17
Totals	87	100	83	100

Orthodox is not very great. Certainly too many members of the two factions owned approximately the same amount of property to warrant any argument based upon a struggle between rich and poor farmers.

Comparison of nonfarm population reveals little difference between Hicksite and Orthodox Friends. Approximately thirty per cent of each group were engaged in nonfarm occupations. The value of the property of these nonfarmers did not vary significantly between Hicksite and Orthodox Friends.

Chester County

HICKSITE

Name	Value of Mill (in $)	Value of Other Property (in $)	Type of Mill
Isaac Pyle	1,800	11,345	?
Isaac Cook	1,600	2,160	Fulling and saw
Lownes Taylor	1,500	5,225	Grist and saw
Benjamin Garrett	1,000	3,600	?
John Pennock	800	200	?
William Thomas	600	2,030	Grist and saw
William Garrett Jr.	550	1,600	Tilt
Mordecai Thomas	450	6,730	Saw and clover
Caleb Maris	375	5,355	Grist and saw
George Garrett	300	7,505	Saw
Ezekiel Webb	300	2,450	Saw
James Pusey	300	2,310	Saw
Thomas Webb	300	5,085	Saw
Thomas Pennock	250	1,385	Saw

ORTHODOX

Name	Value of Mill (in $)	Value of Other Property (in $)	Type of Mill
Isaac Pusey	2,000	3,832	?
Caleb Stroud	1,800	2,330	Grist and saw
John Lewis	1,500	1,805	Grist
Mordecai Larkin	1,000	3,499	Grist and saw
Richard Thomas	600	28,700	?
Enos Thomas	400	4,825	?
John Davis	300	3,965	Grist and saw
John Trimble	300	3,410	?
Robert Garrett	275	9,435	Saw
John R. Thomas	200	20,180	Saw
John Baldwin	150	7,235	Saw

OCCUPATIONS: HICKSITE AND ORTHODOX FRIENDS

	Chester County			
	HICKSITE		ORTHODOX	
OCCUPATION	Number	Per cent	Number	Per cent
Farmer	81	70	88	77
Miller	14	12	11	10
Tanner	4	4	1	1
Storekeeper	0	0	2	2
Tailor	1	1	0	0
Schoolmaster	1	1	0	0
Unknown (non-farm)	12	11	13	11
Totals	113	99	115	101

Despite some similarity of farm and nonfarm property holdings among the Friends, Orthodox Quakers were more likely to be engaged in commercial agriculture. One indication of this is the tendency of the Orthodox to own more cattle than the Hicksites. (It seems likely that farmers who possessed four or more mature cattle were selling butter and cheese.)

The data can be presented in another way. Fifty-nine per cent of the farmers owning more than four cattle became Orthodox. Sixty-three per cent of the farmers owning three or less cattle became Hicksites.[12]

A further contrast between Hicksite and Orthodox Friends can be seen by comparing their tendencies to hold mortgages.[13]

The difference is quite strong. Not only were Hicksites more inclined to hold mortgages, they were also more likely to hold critical ones—that is, mortgages which were in effect during the price collapse of 1816–1819. In addition, Hicksite mortgages were somewhat smaller than those of the Orthodox.

NUMBER OF CATTLE: HICKSITE AND ORTHODOX FARMERS

Delaware County

Number of Mature Cattle	HICKSITE		ORTHODOX	
	Number	Per cent	Number	Per cent
1–3	25	58	13	39
4–5	10	23	6	18
6–	8	19	14	42
Totals	43	100	33	99

Chester County

Number of Mature Cattle	HICKSITE		ORTHODOX	
	Number	Per cent	Number	Per cent
1–3	58	66	35	42
4–5	14	16	25	30
6–	16	18	24	29
Totals	88	100	84	101

MORTGAGES: HICKSITE AND ORTHODOX FRIENDS

Delaware and Chester Counties

	Hicksite	Orthodox
Number checked	194	149
Number mortgaged	60	27
Per cent mortgaged	31	18
Number of critical mortgages	25	10
Per cent of critical mortgages	13	7

SIZE OF MORTGAGES: HICKSITE AND ORTHODOX FRIENDS

Delaware and Chester Counties

SIZE OF MORTGAGE	HICKSITE		ORTHODOX	
(in $)	Number	Per cent	Number	Per cent
1–499	17	29	0	0
500–999	8	14	6	22
1000–1999	15	25	9	33
2000–2999	4	7	4	15
3000–	15	25	8	30
Totals	59	100	27	100

Also interesting is the probability that a higher percentage of Orthodox Friends used their mortgages for commercial purposes. Three-quarters of the Orthodox farm-mortgagees were probably engaged in commercial agriculture. Only about two-fifths of the Hicksite farm-mortgagees were similarly employed.

MORTGAGEES: CHESTER AND DELAWARE COUNTIES

Characteristics	HICKSITE		ORTHODOX	
	Number	Per cent	Number	Per cent
Farm	28	70	17	71
Nonfarm	12	30	7	29
Farmers owning 3 or less cattle	15	54	4	24
Farmers owning 4 or more cattle	13	45	13	76

All the data tend to confirm the sect-church concept. There is contrast in both the amounts and types of property owned by Hicksite and Orthodox Friends and in their tendencies toward such activities as commercial farming. Orthodox Friends were more likely to be engaged in commercial agriculture. They were less likely to be debtors, but when they did borrow money, they were more inclined to use it for commercial purposes.

All these characteristics suggest that Orthodox Friends were not highly alienated from the world. Indeed, they would seem to have been committed to the acquisitive values of society around them. Hicksite characteristics suggest that they were not caught up in the world to the same extent. Their values were more likely to be noncommercial. They were more inclined to be hurt by economic change. Their alienation from the world should have been high.

The validity of the sect-church concept is further confirmed by other evidence. One of the keys to understanding the non-urban Separation lies in the identification of Orthodoxy with Philadelphia and more specifically with well-to-do (sometimes wealthy) urban-dwelling Friends. Orthodox leaders were not the sort of people who would be congenial to many nonurban Friends. Orthodox leaders lived in a cultural and social environment which was foreign to Friends outside the city. In the 1820's antiurban sentiment was strong. Anti-Masonry with its egalitarianism and opposition to cities reflects the sort of belief which would have worked against the Philadelphia Orthodox Leaders. An 1825 issue of the *Anti-Masonic Register* (West Chester, Pennsylvania) portrayed men like the Philadelphia leaders as exploiters of hard-working farmers. It is no accident that Hicksite propaganda referred to such Orthodox leaders as Jonathan Evans and Samuel Bettle as former Masons.[14]

If, on the one hand, Orthodox leaders had little attraction for nonurban Friends, Elias Hicks had a great deal. Hicks's appeal was doubly strong in areas outside the city. He was a farmer who used rural images in his sermons. He appealed to rural people as one of their own—a devout and kindly tiller of the soil.

Hicks's personal qualities undoubtedly caused his listeners to be deaf to his sometimes eccentric doctrine. Details of doctrine were difficult to follow in lengthy oral messages and Hicks's eccentricities were frequently hidden in and among traditional language and images.

Some, probably many, rural Friends saw Hicks as a preserver of eighteenth century quietist ideals. Given Hicks's emphasis on the Inner Light, this was not altogether implausible. William Lippincott, a Quaker farmer from New Jersey, is typical of this Hicksite-quietist view. Lippincott was unquestionably a quietist. In his *Journal,* he describes his efforts to overcome the creature. We must make "an early and full surrender of the will of the creature . . . to the Creator. . . . A total surrender of our wills to His Will." At the same time, Lippincott defended Hicks against the Philadelphia elders. He accused the elders of "slanderous" conduct. After listening to a sermon by Hicks in 1823, Lippincott commented that it was "to my entire satisfaction . . . [Hicks was] divinely favoured in a Remarkable Manner which I thought exceeded Any Thing of this Kind I have Lately, If Ever, seen." Lippincott clearly identified Hicks's ideas with his own quietist views.[15]

Hicks also appealed to some rural Friends through his antimodern secular views. His opposition to schools and such forces for social change as turnpike, canal, and railroad building undoubtedly attracted a considerable following among traditional, conservative rural people but such views severely antagonized others. Many commercial farmers must have been appalled by Hicks's attitude toward internal improvements.

Perhaps most significant of Hicks's secular ideas was his strong antiurban bias. Hicks saw cities as centers of worldliness and idle luxury. He wrote in his *Journal:* "What a vast portion of the joys and comforts of life do the idle and slothful deprive themselves of, by running into cities and towns to avoid laboring in the field." [16]

Despite his appeal, too much emphasis should not be placed

directly on Hicks. Hicksites were not simply followers of Elias Hicks. Many Friends undoubtedly became Hicksites because they were opposed to Orthodoxy and the Orthodox leaders, not because they were drawn to Elias Hicks and his ideas. However, it is important that Hicks did not offend these Friends. Perhaps the best way to interpret the roles of Hicks and the Orthodox leaders is in terms of the reactions which each would have provoked. Each possessed the capacity to attract and repel. The problem is who would be attracted and who repelled?

Given the strength of the factors working against nonurban Orthodoxy it is no wonder that Hicksites were in a large majority outside Philadelphia. Yet there were many nonurban Orthodox Friends. Despite all the pressures to the contrary, these Friends must have felt little or no antagonism toward the values of the city and must have believed that Elias Hicks was preaching erroneous doctrines.

Much of the appeal of Orthodoxy for nonurban Friends must be attributed to an unconscious need which some Friends felt for a religion which would be congenial with their participation in commercial agriculture. Orthodoxy certainly was. Hicks's ideas were not. Traditional Quakerism was, at best, ambivalent. Thus, the attraction of Orthodoxy.

Place of residence also seems to have had some influence on the tendency to become Orthodox. Friends in and around towns and centers of commerce showed a strong inclination toward Orthodoxy. For example, a majority of Friends who lived in the villages of West Chester, Downingtown, and Chester joined the Orthodox branch. Similar pockets of Orthodoxy existed around the Quaker boarding school at Westtown and in Upper Darby in the outskirts of Philadelphia.[17]

Most of these centers of Orthodoxy were in areas where their residents would be in close and continuous contact with non-Friends. This may account for some of the sensitivity to doctrine shown by Orthodox Friends. Orthodox sentiment was strong among non-Friends. Methodists were especially active in Chester and Delaware counties in 1810–1830. They both conducted revival meetings and established permanent churches in areas around Philadelphia. They also accused the Society of Friends of being a center of heterodox belief. To the extent that Orthodox Friends desired to participate in the world, they might well have wanted to endorse a program of doctrine which was popular among the world's people.

In addition to promoting interchange with non-Friends, residence in centers of commerce increased contact with Philadelphia, the center of Orthodoxy within the Society. Westtown School in Chester County had a similar effect. Set up in the late eighteenth century, Westtown quickly became a proper place for young Friends to be educated. The school drew pupils from Philadelphia as well as the countryside. The children of Thomas P. Cope, Thomas Stewardson, Jonathan Evans and other wealthy Orthodox leaders went to Westtown. Furthermore, control of the school was in the hands of these same men. The board of managers contained all of the important Philadelphia Orthodox Friends. Many nonurban Orthodox leaders were also affiliated with the school. Westtown apparently mitigated differences between urban and nonurban Friends and facilitated the growth of Orthodoxy.[18]

The appeal of Orthodoxy outside the city of Philadelphia seems, then, to have been greatest among those Friends who had ties with the outer world. Such ties might be occupational (commercial farming), residential (living in West Chester or Chester), or institutional (Westtown School) but their existence was widespread. Conversely, those Friends who did not have connections with the outer world and whose orientation was essentially local usually became Hicksites.[19]

Inertia, neutrality and ambivalence also brought nonurban Friends into Orthodox and Hicksite folds. One of the crucial struggles between Hicksite and Orthodox Friends was for control of meetinghouses. A small, active, highly motivated minority could capture a meetinghouse. In some cases this actually happened. It was easier for a member of that meeting to continue to worship in the same place. If he was not highly motivated, he might be unwilling to put forth the effort necessary to find a new place to worship. It seems likely that possession of the meetinghouse brought with it the attendance of some passive members. This would partially account for the choices of Hicksite and Orthodox Friends who do not seem to fit the general characteristics of their respective groups.

*   *   *

All the evidence tends to confirm the sect-church concept. Factors influencing urban and nonurban Friends vary but the characteristic pattern of values and alienation among the members of the Hicksite and Orthodox factions do not. The Hicksite-Orthodox Separation was a result of an argument about sect and church.

V. The Rise of Orthodoxy

The simplicity of the sect-church concept should not obscure the complex social and psychological needs which led Friends to accept Orthodox beliefs. It is important, then, to look at the rise of Orthodoxy in more detail.

In general, the Orthodox movement was a homogeneous one. Yet like all social movements, there were variations within it. Let us look first at its leaders. The wealth of these men by itself must have drawn them toward Orthodoxy, but the kind of property which they owned was also an influencing factor. Many of the leaders were engaged in speculative enterprise, that is, economic activity which brought returns without directly involving physical labor. In 1808, Samuel Bettle bought $10,000 to $12,000 worth of clothing in New York and wrote to his wife that he was sure that the simple act of bringing his purchases to Philadelphia would involve great profits. Jonathan Evans speculated in land. He owned farm land in Delaware County, Pennsylvania, worth $16,000, and four houses and eleven lots in Philadelphia. Income from these holdings was large enough to support Evans and his family. More revealing are the wills of the Orthodox leaders. More than 70 per cent of them had sizable holdings in stocks and bonds. For example, Thomas Stewardson's will listed some $61,000 worth of commercial paper. Stewardson had interests in:

Stock:

Bank of North America (31 shares)	$ 9,300.00
Bank of Pennsylvania (22 shares)	5,720.00
Schuylkill Navigation Company (100 shares)	5,100.00
Newmarket Manufacturing Company (25 shares)	25,000.00
Chesapeake and Delaware Canal Company (1 share)	15.00

Bonds:

Lehigh Navigation Company	2,307.00
Philadelphia County	425.00

Loans:

Personal loans and interest due	13,761.00
Total value	$61,628.00

He also owned some 26,000 acres of land in western Pennsylvania.[1]

Stewardson's case is not entirely typical. Some leaders did not own as much speculative property as he did but they nevertheless held similar types of property. The Cope family (Thomas P., Henry, and Israel) had wide holdings in stock as did Samuel P. Griffiths, Ellis Yarnall, Richard Humphreys, and Thomas Wistar. Traditional Quakerism frowned on this sort of economic activity. The Protestant Ethic was strong in Quakerism but it could scarcely be construed as sanctioning speculative enterprise.

The nature of the holdings of Orthodox Friends also suggests a strong interest in the economic revolution going on in early nineteenth century America. Thomas Stewardson, Thomas P. Cope, and others were active in manufacturing and turnpike, canal, and railroad construction. For men in pursuit of wealth and power the changes taking place offered repeated opportunities to fulfill their ambitions. Such opportunities stimulated desires, but Quakerism, particularly traditional quietism and the new Quakerism of Elias Hicks, told men to suppress creaturely desires, to reject the ways of the world and to cultivate the spirit within. This sort of religious belief denied access to alluring and abundant opportunity. For some men the lure of opportunity was irresistible.[2]

This is not to argue that Orthodox Friends ignored all religious restrictions on their economic behavior. They did not. Their publication, *The Friend,* repeatedly urged its readers to temper business activity with a Christian spirit. However, the contents of some articles in *The Friend* suggest that its advice was not always taken.[3]

> Moderation in trade or business does not now mean what was once understood by it; but is taken to signify as large a business as a man can conduct *profitably* by devoting himself to it with all the diligence and alacrity of which he is capable; and the more money he makes, the more fully he is satisfied that he is really doing a very prudent, safe, honest business.

However much Orthodox Friends may have departed from some facets of Quaker tradition, they did not become irresponsible entrepreneurs. They put both their time and their wealth to good use. They were deeply committed to the idea of stewardship. All the wealthy Orthodox leaders willed some of their estates to benevolent purposes and most of them were generous contributors to the public welfare before their deaths. They were active in civic affairs. Orthodox leaders saw themselves as able, intelligent men and felt it their duty to lead society—not just Quakers—along proper paths. Their sense of responsibility and duty was admirable in an age when these traits were all too often missing.[4]

If, on the one hand, the leaders found Orthodoxy attractive because of their economic interests, they were also drawn to it because of its general acceptance among their non-Quaker peers. During the early nineteenth century the enthusiasm of non-Friends for Orthodoxy frequently led them to attack Quakerism as a center of un-Christian doctrine. Some Friends responded to these attacks by defending traditional Quaker emphases upon continuous revelation, experience, and the Inner Light. Orthodox leaders responded by saying that

Friends were just as Orthodox as anyone else—or at least true
Friends were.

Orthodox leaders went to great lengths to prove their Orthodoxy to non-Friends. Their concern about the opinions
of people outside the Society was partially, perhaps primarily,
due to their own social insecurities. Most of the Orthodox
leaders had risen in social position during their lives. They
had achieved upward mobility. Upward mobility is generally
accompanied by anxiety. A newly arrived individual must
explore his position. He must acclimatize himself to its values
and patterns of behavior. He is likely to have feelings of
"normlessness," that is, an absence of accepted internalized
standards. Upwardly mobile persons are usually sensitive to
public opinion and particularly the opinions of their social
peers. For upwardly mobile Friends, Orthodoxy was attractive for just this reason. It was popular. It was a proper form
of belief.[5]

The social insecurities of Orthodox leaders may also account for their hypersensitivity to challenges to their position
within the Society. If this is true, then the vehement Orthodox responses to outsiders like Elias Hicks become more
understandable. Hicks's challenge to them was social as well
as doctrinal. Jonathan Evans's description of his break with
Elias Hicks in 1819 seems to sustain this view. At that time,
Evans did not object to Hicks's lack of Orthodoxy. Evans was
upset because Hicks had insulted the Philadelphia leaders.
Hicks, wrote Evans, "incited the youth" against their elders
and maintained that "the whole head [of the Society] was sick
and no soundness in it."[6]

Orthodox leaders left little written evidence of their social
anxieties. Hicksites, however, frequently pointed out the importance of social factors. John Cockburn, in his description
of the Separation, suggests that "the ardour and restiveness
of the Orthodox leaders will be in proportion as their importance and standing seem to be affected." Cockburn says

that the Orthodox gained status by being leaders in the Society of Friends. Benjamin Ferris, a perceptive Hicksite leader, describes the Orthodox as "new rich." Comments of this kind ought not to be taken at face value. They were useful in mobilizing anti-Orthodox sentiment. Yet their prevalence lends support to the idea of social anxiety among the Orthodox.[7]

Orthodoxy grew as a result of the efforts of an elite. It was not a spontaneous popular movement. Many Friends may have been inclined toward Orthodoxy but the activities of a few leaders gave it concrete form. These leaders, driven by the pressures of wealth, speculation, opportunity, mobility and social anxiety, found Orthodoxy an especially congenial form of worship. They then sought to spread Orthodoxy to the point where it was accepted by the Society as a whole.

Those who followed the leaders were not as seriously affected by these pressures but were rather influenced by some which were not widely felt by the leaders. Orthodox followers did not entirely escape socioeconomic pressures. The quantitative examination of Orthodox Friends in Chapters II and III demonstrates that in some respects their social and psychological needs would not be met by traditional Quakerism. To this extent Orthodox followers were subject to the same kinds of tensions as their leaders. They were not highly alienated; they wished to live in the world and accept its values, yet they belonged to a religion which emphasized rejection of the world and its goods.

Followers were attracted for other reasons as well. Some were probably influenced by the imposing stature of the Orthodox leaders. Men like Thomas Stewardson, Richard Humphreys, Joseph Scattergood, and Thomas P. Cope commanded respect. Cope's achievements as shipping magnate, politician, civic leader, social reformer, and friend of Stephen Girard lent prestige to his religious views. Such achievements gave an aura of respectability to Orthodoxy. They attracted anyone who attached significance to success as defined by the secular world.[8]

Family, friendship, business ties, and place of residence also pulled Friends toward (and away from) Orthodoxy. Tradition and habit inclined urban Friends to become Orthodox and nonurban ones to become Hicksites. Lines of division were also drawn within these two regions. Orthodox Friends lived near one another. Nearly 60 per cent of a randomly chosen group of Orthodox Friends in Philadelphia lived in the area bounded by Front, Cherry, High (Market), and Schuylkill Fourth streets. Forty-five per cent of the same group lived on or near Mulberry (Arch) Street.[9]

Proximity alone would have caused Orthodox Friends to be acquainted with one another but their relationship was deeper than mere proximity. They were often intimate friends. Their interests were congenial. They were concerned about each other's problems. They worried together about their children, illness, and financial problems. They visited each other's homes. In short, they had close personal bonds which had no direct connection with their religious views.

Family and business association promoted additional ties. Orthodox Friends did business with one another. They were each other's customers, suppliers, partners, money lenders, advisers, importers and exporters. Here again, there was both common interest and regular face-to-face contact. If family ties are added to the bonds of residence, business, common interest, and regular contact, the nature of Orthodox unity becomes apparent. Friends married other Friends. Naturally they tended to marry within their own social circles. Proximity of residence encouraged this tendency. The network of intermarriage was complex but it did not often cross what soon became the division between Hicksite and Orthodox Friends. Whether Hicksite or Orthodox, primary families seldom split.[10]

For passive Friends, for Friends who would not have precipitated a Separation, for Friends who were not profoundly affected by such things as upward mobility and social insecurity, the bonds of family, friendship, business and residence were often crucial. When passive Friends were forced to choose between Hicksite and Orthodox branches, these factors pushed them in one direction or the other. In some cases there were pressures in both directions, but generally this was not true. For most Friends the decision, however difficult, was clearcut. They did not seriously consider any alternatives.

* * *

Friends who found Orthodoxy attractive picked it up from many sources. Since Orthodoxy was in the air, it is fruitless to try to identify its origins too precisely. Nevertheless it seems likely that the primary source of Orthodox sentiment was English Quakerism. By the late eighteenth century, English Friends had become strongly Orthodox. American Friends were in regular contact with England. Many of the active Orthodox ministers had traveled in England and English ministers had, in turn, visited America. Between 1790 and 1827 twenty English ministers came to America and seventeen ministers from Philadelphia Yearly Meeting went to England. This interchange could not help but introduce American Friends to Orthodoxy.

American visitors to England and their friends often became Orthodox leaders. Jonathan Evans's father-in-law and Joseph Scattergood's father were both in England between 1790 and 1799. Richard Jordan and William Jackson visited England between 1800 and 1809. Only one future Hicksite, Jesse Kersey, made the journey to England in the forty years preceding the Separation.

Orthodox Friends were generally sympathetic toward English products and ideas. For them, English goods possessed prestige simply because of their origin. Orthodox Friends were frequently importers and thus had business ties in England. Naturally, then, English forms of worship would hold a certain amount of attraction.[11]

This is not to say that English Friends *caused* the growth of Orthodoxy in America. They did not. It means only that English Quakerism offered an alternative form of belief which some American Friends found congenial. The beliefs of the English Friends were not much different from Orthodox sentiment among non-Friends in America but their organization and techniques of worship were. Some American Friends might find Orthodox doctrines attractive but they could not accept the religious enthusiasm and use of ministers in other American Protestant groups. English Quakerism offered acceptable doctrine without distasteful forms of worship.[12]

It is also difficult to establish a time for the beginning of Orthodoxy. Such movements do not, of course, have precise beginnings, but it is possible to place the origin of Orthodoxy somewhere in the late seventeen nineties. The period from 1790 to 1810 seems to have been a trying one for the eventual Orthodox leaders. They repeatedly remarked on "the low state of the Society." Jonathan Evans described the situation in pessimistic terms. "The awful query," he wrote in 1802, "is *where is the improvement,* the prospect of which . . . is so gloomy, that on looking over things and the state of the society, I am ready to exclaim, 'what will become of us?' " [13]

Taken alone, Evans's comment is not of much importance. Friends frequently made such statements. However, Orthodox leaders repeated this theme so many times that it does seem significant. All the eventual Orthodox leaders saw the early nineteenth century as a critical period in the development of Quakerism. It is highly probable that it was during this self-conceived period of crisis that Orthodoxy first gained influence. In any case, by 1815 there were many Friends who had vaguely and unknowingly committed themselves to Orthodoxy. There is no evidence that these Friends were, as yet, seeking to impose their views upon the rest of the Society but they did control most of the positions of influence within Philadelphia Yearly Meeting.

Two factors pushed Orthodox Friends toward awareness and organization of their beliefs. The increased tempo of religious controversy in New England and the appearance of Elias Hicks in Philadelphia both forced them to clarify their religious position. Orthodoxy antedated antagonism between Elias Hicks and the Elders in 1819, but Orthodox adherents were not well organized nor were their beliefs well formed. Orthodox Friends were not aware that they were doing something new.

Once Hicks appeared in Philadelphia the situation changed rapidly. He made Orthodox Friends aware of their views. He forced them to think through their ideas and to organize in order to perpetuate their influence. After 1820, Orthodox Friends were both organized and conscious of their religious ideas. They were also convinced that Hicks and men like him threatened the very foundation of true Christian religion— that is, the tenets of the Orthodox creed.

Orthodox fears were heightened by events in New England. Beginning about 1815 an anti-Orthodox New Light movement broke out among Friends in Eastern Massachusetts. This, coupled with the Unitarian schism in the Congregational Church, was enough to convince Orthodox Friends in Philadelphia that the forces of infidelity were not to be taken lightly.[14]

Throughout the controversy, Orthodox adherents focused their attentions on doctrinal issues. They were sure that their own position was the only one which a true Christian could take. They interpreted all criticisms as part of a Hicksite "conspiracy." Hicks's influence, they thought, extended as far as Ohio and Indiana. One Orthodox Friend even thought he had found a Hicksite organization in Canada.[15]

In placing so much emphasis on Hicks and his ideas, Orthodox Friends misunderstood the nature of the opposition to them. The Hicksite movement was not simply an attempt to spread the ideas of Elias Hicks. There never was a unified Hicksite party. Nevertheless, the Orthodox acted upon the basis of truth as they saw it and, as far as they were concerned, there was a well organized and dangerous Hicksite party.

*   *   *

The rise of Orthodoxy among the Friends is best seen as the result of the efforts of a small group of men who had grown restive under the restraints of traditional Quaker belief and practice. The pattern of social and psychological need and personal ties among Friends was such that many of them were receptive to the doctrinal alternatives offered by this small group of leaders.

When the doctrines and influence of the leaders were challenged by what they thought was a threat to true Christianity, the leaders sought to solidify their control and extend their influence throughout Philadelphia Yearly Meeting. Their successes prompted the growth of opposition and eventually resulted in the Separation of 1827.

VI. Hicksite Responses

Probably the best way to interpret the Hicksite movement is as a heterogeneous response to Orthodoxy. Those Quakers became Hicksites who were in some way alienated by Orthodox leaders, activities, and beliefs. In this respect, the unity of the Hicksites was negative. They agreed on opposition to something, though not clearly defined.

One source of alienation from Orthodoxy was the personal characteristics of the Orthodox leaders. Orthodox leaders were vulnerable to social enmity. They were wealthy, refined, urban-dwelling businessmen. These characteristics, regardless of the doctrines associated with them, would have made Orthodox leaders the subject of considerable suspicion. To rural Friends, the Orthodox leaders represented the corrupting influence of the city. To urban-dwelling artisans they were members of a nonproducing privileged class which was just then being widely criticized. To affluent, established Friends like Clement Biddle and William Wharton, the Orthodox represented the new rich. All these antagonisms were present at the time of the Separation and all of them can be found in Hicksite writings both before and after the actual split of 1827. In this sense, some of the antipathy toward the Orthodox leaders can be attributed to their social characteristics.[1]

It is also significant that at this time awareness of social position was heightened by the growth of a widely influential egalitarian ideology. This ideology attacked privilege and inequality in all forms. Because it emphasized social differences, it tended to act as a wedge between the various levels of society. Within the Society of Friends, it made Friends increasingly conscious of social issues. Some Hicksites found the idea of egalitarianism useful. They argued that the Separation represented a struggle between the good people and the evil aristocrats—between aristocracy and democracy. Although urban in origin, this sort of thinking also affected the views of rural and semi-rural Friends. It certainly supplemented urban resentment of the well-to-do and rural suspicion of the city. It also closely resembled traditional Quaker emphasis upon man's equality before God. In this sense, the Hicksite movement takes on another dimension as part of a widely pervasive egalitarian impulse, comparable perhaps to the contemporary Anti-Masonic crusade in New York.[2]

The wedge between various segments of the Society was driven even deeper by the general religious ferment of the period. Religious enthusiasm ran high in the early nineteenth century. It exerted strong pressure on Quaker tradition through both written and oral denunciations of the Society of Friends and thus it added to the uneasiness developing within the Society. Furthermore, it offered a variety of religious alternatives at a time when many Friends were restive under restraints imposed by eighteenth century quietism.[3]

In general, ferment outside the Society provided a frame of reference through which participants in the Separation could understand their role in that struggle. The Hicksite-Orthodox schism should not be equated with the Unitarian controversy in New England yet it is important to realize that both Quaker groups saw their differences as being analogous to those in New England. Therefore, one should be aware of a positive interaction between the Hicksites and the Uni-

tarians as well as the negative one between Hicksite and
Orthodox. This is not to call the Hicksites Unitarians but
rather to suggest that there was a largely unconscious interchange of values and ideas between the two groups.[4]

The tactics of the Orthodox leaders were also a source of
alienation. Orthodox efforts to control and change the Society
of Friends frequently took the form of personal attacks upon
Friends who disagreed with them. Elias Hicks was the most
important of the individuals subjected to these attacks, but he
was by no means the only one. To some extent, the word
"attack" is too strong, for the Orthodox usually remained
within traditions of privacy and brotherly love. On the other
hand, they sometimes ignored these limitations and engaged
in vindictive and insulting harangues upon other members
of the Society, breaking with both propriety and tradition in
doing so.

Early nineteenth century Quakerism represented a closely
knit community. Business, friendship, and marriage all were
circumscribed by the bounds of the Society. Thus an attack
upon any single individual inevitably involved Friends who
had no direct connection with the issues involved, but who
were friends of the individual, friends of his relatives, relatives of his friends, and so on.

This complex network of personal relationships undoubtedly had a strong influence on the course of the Separation.
For example, all the eventual Hicksite leaders were friends
of Elias Hicks before the first attack was made upon him in
1819, but they did not all endorse his doctrinal opinions.
Furthermore, they were all mutual friends at that time. Many
of them had lived near one another in Philadelphia, had attended Meeting together, and were also related by marriage.
To be sure, some families and friends were split by the Separation but the percentage thus affected was extremely small.[5]

The religious views of the Orthodox were, however, the
most significant source of alienation. Especially important

in this respect was the widespread belief that Orthodox doctrine represented a serious departure from Quaker tradition. Orthodox emphases were clearly something new and to some members of the Society newness was anathema. Friends like Samuel Comfort, Halliday Jackson, and John Comly wished to preserve the past. They resented efforts to introduce changes in Quaker organization and belief. These men might well be termed traditionalists since they looked to the past and to quietism for their values. They were traditional in another sense too, for they resisted secular changes as well as religious ones. Even in temperament they appear to have been conservative.

The traditionalism of Halliday Jackson and Samuel Comfort is not difficult to explain. Both had chosen farming as an occupation after brief periods as teachers. Both were small farmers who did not prosper economically. Both were suspicious of the city and its values and believed in the virtues of an agricultural way of life. Both were active in social reform. Quietism was well suited to their needs. Orthodoxy was not. Thus the two men sought to preserve their old beliefs in the face of Orthodox deviation. Much of the rural and semi-rural support for the Hicksites was undoubtedly of this Jackson-Comfort variety.[6]

The case of John Comly is more complex. Comly was a teacher and author who spent much of his adult life in Byberry in the outskirts of Philadelphia. Never wealthy, Comly was, nevertheless, economically secure. Despite his occupation, Comly does not seem to have had an active, volatile mind. His *Journal* had a solid, flat quality which is probably a reflection of Comly himself. Comly does not seem to have seriously entered into the controversy between Hicks and the elders until just prior to the split in 1827, nor does he seem to have been deeply concerned about the ideas involved.

Comly would not of himself have precipitated a split. He wanted to resolve peacefully a dilemma which already existed and was the result of the immoderate activities of others. Comly saw himself in the role of a healer. He says in his *Journal* that he favored Separation because he deplored controversy. He wished to preserve the decorum of Meeting—to do things in a proper Quaker manner. He also points to Orthodox efforts to gain control of Yearly Meeting as the primary source of contention. Comly thus reveals himself as a temperamental conservative. In the eighteenth century he had committed himself to the then dominant quietist view. He was not about to change his mind in middle age. He resented Orthodox tinkering as something new and as an unnecessary intrusion into Meeting. Comly wished to return Quakerism to the tranquility of eighteenth century quietism and the only way he could envision doing so was to secede from Orthodox control. This was his quiet retreat from a scene of confusion.[7]

Hicksite support was not all rural nor all conservative; other sources of Hicksite antagonism to Orthodoxy are to be found. Within the cities, the Hicksites were strongly supported by people whose occupations and incomes placed them in middle and lower positions in society. There were cabinetmakers like Abraham Lower, laborers like Isaac Townsend, and such voiceless figures as James Boustead (currier), George Coffee (sprig cutter), James Conway (blacksmith), Samuel G. Cole (tailor), and Samuel Haydock (plumber). In all, some 40 per cent of Philadelphia Hicksites were artisans. These artisans form a second group within the Hicksite movement—a group which might well be called sectarian in that its members felt a need to preserve Quaker emphases upon works and a behavioral code.

James Mott, an active Hicksite, is representative of the sectarians. Struggle as he might, Mott could not achieve material success. After working (and failing) in several business ventures, Mott wrote to his parents: [8]

Happy is the man who has a good farm clear of debt, and
is therewith content, and does not know how to write his
name! A person thus situated knows little of the anxiety
attendant upon a mercantile life, when perhaps the hard
earnings of many anxious days and sleepless nights are
swept away by failures and losses on almost every hand.
I say to those who have been brought up in the country,
stay there.

Mott's anxiety about his secular affairs was undoubtedly
repeated in the minds of many of the Philadelphia artisans.
If one can judge by the labor movement in Philadelphia in
the eighteen twenties, artisans in the city were undergoing
considerable strain in their secular lives. Often they were being by-passed by socioeconomic change and, as a result, felt
insecure in the face of the impermanence which surrounded
them. It is natural that Hicksite artisans might seek outlets
for their insecurities within the sectarian orientation of the
Society of Friends, and that they found the Society's emphasis
on behavior and rejection of the world's values particularly
comforting.

The values to which these sectarian Friends attached so
much importance were precisely the ones which the Orthodox had found uncomfortable and were trying to change.
Thus, those Friends who felt a need for a sectarian religion
were alienated from Orthodoxy because it weakened the barrier between Friends and the world.

The object of these sectarians, like that of the traditionalists, was primarily conservative, an effort to cling to the ways
of the past. These two groups—sectarian and traditionalist—
made up the bulk of support for the Hicksite movement. The
religious beliefs of the two groups were similar but their
motivations were not.

Orthodox doctrine and organization disturbed yet another
group of Friends who felt that Orthodoxy in general represented a serious threat to religious liberalism. These religious

liberals—men like Benjamin Ferris, Joseph Parrish, Clement Biddle, John Moore, and William Gibbons—were highly vocal and thus exerted an influence out of proportion to their small numbers. They were interested in reform and the future and possessed temperaments which were both broadly tolerant and congenial to change. Perhaps more important, they had a deep faith in the possibility of improving the human condition and felt a responsibility to do so.[9]

For some of the liberals, motivation seems to have come from a commitment to principles of tolerance and free inquiry. Benjamin Ferris is the best example of such an individual, but other liberals seem to have been similarly motivated. Benjamin Ferris was a versatile man. Born in Wilmington in 1780, Ferris was apprenticed to a Philadelphia watchmaker when he was fourteen. While learning a trade, he spent most of his time reading and talking. In addition to American and English subjects, Ferris became interested in France and the French Revolution and apparently spent some time talking with French émigrés.[10]

Ferris remained in Philadelphia almost twenty years and then, in 1813, moved to Wilmington where he made his home until his death in 1867. The years spent in Philadelphia were important ones. The intellectual environment was certainly stimulating, and Ferris's brilliance found outlets in the city which might otherwise have been unavailable. His later activities as artist, poet, and historian undoubtedly stem from this period.

While in Philadelphia Ferris also formed lasting personal ties. He attended Green Street Meeting, which later became the center of the Hicksite movement in the city, and made friends with people who were to be active in the Hicksite cause. The extent of these personal ties is difficult to determine, but given Ferris's outgoing, personable manner it seems likely that his range of acquaintance was broad.

Ferris's temperament was not such that he was long content

with watchmaking and once in Wilmington he took up conveyancing and surveying. Ferris must have been skilled at his work for he quickly accumulated a small fortune and, in 1835, he retired. He spent the last thirty years of his life studying and writing.

Above all else, Benjamin Ferris was a man of principle. He refused to vote for President because the President was Commander-in-Chief of the Army (all men should live in peace; a vote for President was an endorsement of war). He was active in efforts to aid the Indian, Negro, blind, and deaf and dumb (all men were equal and important in the eyes of God). He rejected invitations to enter into money seeking business ventures (the affairs of the world should not assume priority in men's affairs).

Some of Ferris's strongest commitments were to liberal, rational (but not Deistic) theology, tolerance of diversity, and freedom of inquiry. His opposition to Orthodoxy stems from these commitments. He felt that Orthodox Friends were intolerant, opposed free inquiry and accepted religious doctrines which were wholly irrational. Thus his opposition to Orthodoxy.

Convenient and accurate as this explanation of Ferris's behavior may be, it leaves the reasons for his commitment to principles unexplained. Why did he believe in principles? Why in some principles and not others? The answers to these questions are hidden within the inner self of Benjamin Ferris. He and those like him were the "altruists" of the Hicksite movement.

Like Ferris, other liberals saw Orthodoxy as a threat to their values and commitments. They feared that a vast and conspiratorial attempt was being made to destroy religious freedom in the United States. Evangelical organizations were attempting to build a Christian political party. The evangelists sought to control the schools; they formed Bible and tract societies; they sent out missionaries. In short, it seemed

to the liberals as if certain religious organizations were trying to destroy freedom of conscience.[11]

Liberal fears increased when the Society of Friends became
the subject of evangelical attacks from outside, but they were
even more upset when those attacks began to come from
sources inside the Society. The response of the Hicksite liberals to the Orthodox group was, then, only one phase of their
general response to what the liberals felt was a broadly based
dogmatism and intolerance. The struggle of Quaker liberals
was a continuation of a struggle which had begun much
earlier and had been directed toward the preservation of
religious freedom in America.[12]

On the whole, liberal objections to the growth of Orthodoxy among Friends were based upon their concern for
tolerance and freedom of worship. Liberals felt that all men
had the right to believe and worship as they wished. All men
should be guaranteed an opportunity to seek religious truth
for themselves. In the mind of the liberals, Elias Hicks had a
right to believe and say whatever his spirit led him to believe
and say.[13]

Nevertheless, liberals were not content with general statements of principle. They also launched a direct attack upon
Orthodox doctrine. Specifically, the liberals denied the validity of the Bible as a guide to God's unchanging revelation, of
the concept of Christ's atonement, and the idea of the Trinity.
Liberal arguments against the Orthodox creed show that they
were familiar with such European religious scholars as Johann
Mosheim (1694–1755) and also with the concepts and techniques of comparative religion. However, the primary basis
for their attacks upon Orthodox doctrine was not European
scholarship. Rather, it was their belief that communion between man and God was continuous and that this communion
could be pursued individually through the spiritual union of
the meeting. The spirit of God was in all men. Neither Christ
nor priest, neither creed nor ceremony was the key to salva-

tion. That, they thought, was contained in the spirit within, the Inner Light.[14]

Liberal belief in the Inner Light was directly connected with faith in the perfectibility of man. If the spirit within could be cultivated to the point where it controlled the actions of men, it would be possible for men to create a good society here on earth—a society dedicated to brotherly love, freedom of conscience, and human equality.[15]

Liberal ideals held their adherents in constant tension between what is and what ought to be. Liberal efforts at social reform were a natural corollary of this tension. Furthermore, the liberal faith in perfectibility caused them to become interested in the secular reform activities of people like Robert Owen and his son, Robert Dale Owen. These secular reform programs were rejected but the liberals did express both interest and sympathy.[16]

If the theme of a response to Orthodoxy is momentarily abandoned and the Hicksites are examined in terms of leaders, active participants, and followers, the importance of liberal influence is apparent. While a few leaders were drawn from among traditionalists and sectarians, it was the liberals who dominated Hicksite leadership. Furthermore, liberals determined the content of the theological response to Orthodoxy through such publications as *The Berean* and exercised preponderant control over anti-Orthodox activities before and after the Separation.

The importance of the liberal leaders should not, however, obscure the profoundly conservative motives of most Hicksite followers. The vast majority of the Hicksites were traditionalists and sectarians and were driven by a desire to preserve old ways of worship.[17]

The complexity of the Hicksite movement did not prevent the development of a religious consensus among its participants. Despite their diverse motivations, Hicksites generally agreed as to the proper character of religious structure and belief. They all desired a loosely knit structure which would preserve the sectarian characteristics of the Society of Friends. This kind of religion would fulfill the needs and aspirations of traditional, liberal, and socially dislocated elements within the movement. All segments accepted an individual religion based on continuous revelation in which cultivation of the inner spirit was emphasized rather than specific outer belief.[18]

The two key elements in the Hicksite synthesis were a weak central organization and an emphasis on behavior, not belief, as a measure of a man's religion. To some extent, Hicksite endeavors to perpetuate a weak organization stemmed from tradition and a belief in equality. They were also a result of a negative reaction to the Orthodox proclivity for centralization. Since Orthodox efforts to manipulate the Society had centered in the Meeting for Sufferings, Select Meetings and Yearly Meeting, Hicksites endeavored to weaken the influence of all these institutions. They sought to decentralize and diffuse power. They tried to take authority away from a hierarchy and place it in the hands of the general membership.

A variety of suggestions were made as to how this sort of organization might be achieved. The strongest recommendation was one which urged the abandonment of the Meeting for Sufferings. Other proposals were made to: 1) limit the term of office for members of the hierarchy, 2) impose the principle of rotation of office, 3) prevent the Meeting for Sufferings and Select Meetings from influencing the choice of their members.[19]

These proposals were not irresponsible criticisms of Orthodox power. In the years immediately following the Separation, the Hicksites did weaken the authority of institutions beyond the local level of the Preparative Meeting. For example, appointments to Yearly Meeting (1828–1832) suggest that a principle of rotation of office was followed. During that short period several hundred representatives were appointed. Most of the representatives received only one appointment out of five and almost no one was appointed for all five of the years. Furthermore, those who did receive several appointments do not seem to have been the most influential members of Yearly Meeting.[20]

The other half of the Hicksite synthesis—an emphasis on behavior—is, perhaps, more important than the desire for a weak central organization. Repeatedly, the Hicksites stressed the importance of behavior, not belief, as a measure of a man's religion. The use of a belief to determine religious qualifications seemed to them to lead to a shallow religion which dealt only with externals. It bred a sterile formality which eased the conscience of the believer without affecting his spiritual improvement. Such a religion allowed its adherents to call themselves holy men without their seeking to become holy.

The Hicksites felt that religion should embody a set of eternal values that its members should seek to fulfill. They stressed the importance of drawing behavioral guides from a religious code rather than from general culture standards. For some Hicksites this emphasis upon a code of behavior probably represented an escape from the world. It did provide a nonsecular frame of reference in which those members who were alienated from the world could find solace and security. Nevertheless, the code also emphasized that a man must live in the world and fulfill his obligations to his fellow man. Those Friends who sincerely adhered to these beliefs were held in a state of tension. The code which they endorsed was not an easy one to live with. Almost every facet of it pointed in two directions at once: a man must work hard but not become too involved in the fruits of his labor; he must reject the values of the world but continue to live in that world and seek to improve it; and he must direct his actions toward unrealizable goals.

The principles contained in the Hicksite consensus were subject to a variety of interpretations. They left the way open for the members of each group to fulfill their own needs in their own way. For example, to traditionalists, they represented a continuation of quietism; to liberals, a basis for tolerance and reform; and to sectarians, a source of relief from secular anxiety. It is also interesting to note that most of the ideas of Elias Hicks fall within the scope of this consensus. Indeed, his ideas seem to have been interpreted in so many ways that liberal and traditional alike could find comfort in them. Hicks's actual role in the Separation is unclear, but it is apparent that he and his ideas were not the primary basis for the movement which took his name. The Hicksite movement was the result of a heterogeneous response to Orthodoxy.

VII. Some Conclusions

Social institutions such as religion are intimately connected with their total environment. Similarly, human beings—participants in social institutions—operate as wholes and inhabit several environments at the same time. This study of the Quakers well illustrates the importance of examining functional relationships between various aspects of the whole; between people's secular lives and their religious needs; between socioeconomic change and religious expression.

Acceptance of this functional view forces departure from methods which rely solely on written evidence and narrative synthesis and requires use of demographic data—census returns, wills, tax records, city directories. It points to the importance of quantification and analytical synthesis. Historians have too long ignored such readily available data and techniques. Through an archaic attachment to "humanism," they neglect human beings who left no written records. Perhaps, after all, social scientists are more interested in real people and real situations; perhaps they are more "humanistic" than the humanists.

The method of collective biography used in this study offers a means for taking persons into account who would normally be excluded and, in doing so, presents a broader interpretive base from which to work. It allows the researcher to come to concrete conclusions about what kinds of people engaged in what kinds of behavior. When used for this purpose, comparative evidence must be presented for it is necessary to identify those characteristics peculiar to individuals under study.

Definition of behavior and unique characteristics may obviate some interpretations and encourage others, but of itself cannot reveal why they are connected. The crucial step in the method of collective biography lies in providing those connectives and this is the task of the researcher. On the basis of characteristics known to him, he must speculate about mental contexts which caused persons to perform certain acts. Even when the researcher is intimately acquainted with social theory and with the material under study, the limitations of such an approach are many, yet certainly they are less than those of traditional history.

For example, students of the Hicksite Separation have long pointed to an urban-rural split between Orthodox and Hicksite Friends. The reasons for this interpretation are not hard to find—participants in the schism were aware of division along these lines and left written evidence supporting their view. Broadly speaking, the split did tend to follow urban-nonurban lines but use of collective biography suggests a need for a more sophisticated interpretive tool than city *versus* country. Similarly, due to the strong emphasis which Orthodox Friends placed on the role of Elias Hicks, Hicksites have generally been interpreted as being his followers. However, quantitative study casts doubt on such a simplistic theory and encourages an interpretive framework which accounts for diversity among Hicks's supposed supporters and seeks to encompass voiceless followers as well as articulate leaders.

Quantification also points to a relatively high degree of unity among Orthodox adherents, especially leaders, and provides means for understanding why some Friends found Orthodoxy attractive. It shows how kinds of wealth and length of possession appear to have led to a state of mind antithetical to sectarianism and how such things as personal and family ties drew Friends to opt for one branch or the other.

The central argument here can be succinctly stated: men act as whole beings. When a merchant went to Friends meeting, he brought the ideals and practices of his mercantile activities along with him. He also brought friendships, and his relationships with his parents, wife, and children. In short, he brought his total life experience; so too did those who sat around him. Any effort to study religion as a social institution must, then, take this totality into account. Religion cannot be abstracted from the whole of which it is an integral part.

A functional approach to this whole provides fruitful insights into relationships between religion and social change. It presents guides for research which lead the historian to look systematically at problems and materials which he might otherwise ignore and cautions him to beware of generalizations based on written descriptions of historical events. It adds new dimensions to old historical problems and opens up areas for research which are virtually unexplored.

Helpful as a functional view may be, it is no guide to absolute truth. It raises questions, suggests possible answers, and provides systematic techniques for seeking those answers. It does not provide *the* answer to any question and what answers it does provide are always in terms of tendency and range. For example, theories drawn from the sociology of religion suggest the general characteristics which Hicksite and Orthodox Quakers "should" have, but can predict neither what any single Hicksite or Orthodox Friend will be like nor what motivated him to join the branch that he did.

A functional view presents other dilemmas. It relies on two key ideas: 1) religion is an attempt to fulfill certain human needs, and 2) human needs stem from the total environment. Human needs exist within the mind. Thus, the historian who accepts a functional view is forced to delve into the inner psyche of individuals who are dead and who acted in a different sociocultural environment. Usually the only bases for judging this inner state of mind are such external factors as mobility, occupation, wealth, residence, and so on. Obviously, conclusions about inner needs which rely on external evidence are highly tenuous even if they are based on quantitative data. Therefore, both evidence and bases for its interpretation must be clearly presented.

At present, however, the greatest problems stem not from shortcomings of technique and evidence but rather from a lack of studies dealing with questions fundamental to any social analysis. We know all too little about American class structure, status ranks, socioeconomic change and occupations, transportation, wages and prices, commercial agriculture, vertical and horizontal mobility—the list could be extended indefinitely. Until basic demographic studies are conducted, research of the kind found in this book will be doubly tenuous. Hopefully, such studies will soon be forthcoming and we can then proceed toward a fuller understanding of the American past and, indeed, of human behavior generally.

This brief description of limitations of technique and knowledge should not be construed as a strategic retreat into traditionalist ranks. It is not. The methods of this study could and should be extended to numerous other social and religious movements. It is fruitless to argue, as we so often do, about abstractions without even knowing what people and what situations we are arguing about. Recent studies which have focused in depth on real people in real situations have already laid open to question many standard clichés of American history. Undoubtedly they will continue to do so. Far from a retreat, the call here is for new advances, more research, and awareness of the merits of sociological knowledge and methods.

Notes

CHAPTER I

1. The following discussion of the sociology of religion is based primarily upon: J. Milton Yinger, *Religion, Society, and the Individual* (New York, 1957); Elizabeth K. Nottingham, *Religion and Society* (New York, 1954); and N. J. Demerath, *Social Class in American Protestanism* (Chicago, 1965).

2. Yinger, *Religion, Society, and the Individual*, 15–16.

3. Ernst Troeltsch, *Social Teachings of the Christian Church*, 2 vols., Torchbook edition (New York, 1960).

4. Yinger, *Religion, Society, and the Individual*, 265.

5. See Seymour M. Lipset, *Political Man*, Anchor edition (New York, 1963), 100.

6. Gerhard Lenski, *The Religious Factor*, revised edition (New York, 1963), 357. Lenski uses the term *socio-religious group* to refer to both communal and associational aspects of membership in religious groups. See pages 18–24.

7. Lenski, *The Religious Factor*, 320; Lee Benson, *The Concept of Jacksonian Democracy*, Atheneum edition (New York, 1964).

8. The following discussion relies heavily upon: Norman F. Washburne, *Interpreting Social Change in America* (New York, 1954); C. Wendell King, *Social Movements in the United States* (New York, 1956); Hadley Cantril, *Psychology of Social Movements* (New York, 1941); and Hans Toch, *The Social Psychology of Social Movements* (New York, 1965).

9. King, *Social Movements*, 32.

10. King, *Social Movements*, 11–24.

11. King, *Social Movements*, 20.

12. Cantril, *Psychology of Social Movements*, 65–77.

13. King, *Social Movements*, 63–64.

14. Emery Battis, *Saints and Sectaries* (Chapel Hill, North Carolina, 1962), 249–285; Cantril, *Psychology of Social Movements*, 144–168.

15. There are levels of functional analysis ranging from a common sense recognition of inter-relatedness to theories which rely on functional prerequisites. Several excellent articles on the strengths and weaknesses of functionalism may be found in Don Martindale (ed.), *Functionalism in the Social Sciences* (Philadelphia, 1965). A middle range functionalism such as that outlined by Robert K. Merton in his *Social Theory and Social Structure* (Glencoe, Illinois, 1957) is likely to be of greatest use to the historian. The level of analysis presented above is roughly equivalent to that of Merton.

CHAPTER II

1. A detailed description of Philadelphia Yearly Meeting in 1827 can be found in William Bacon Evans, *Jonathan Evans* (Boston, 1959).

2. John Comly, *Journal* (Philadelphia, 1853), 319. Much of the following discussion is based on Comly's description of the events which took place during and immediately following Yearly Meeting in 1827.

3. The full text of the address can be found in John Cockburn, *Cockburn's Review* (Philadelphia, 1829), 199–204.

4. Elbert Russell, *The History of Quakerism* (New York, 1942). The best treatment of 18th century Friends is Frederick B. Tolles, *Meeting House and Counting House* (Chapel Hill, North Carolina, 1948). Also important is Howard Brinton, *Friends for 300 Years* (New York, 1952).

5. Tolles, *Meeting House and Counting House*, 234–243.

6. The following discussion of the ideas of Elias Hicks is based on his *Journal* (New York, 1832) and *Sermons* (Philadelphia, 1825). Also useful are Rufus Jones, *The Later Periods of Quakerism* (New York, 1921), I, 444–457 and Bliss Forbush, *Elias Hicks, Quaker Liberal* (New York, 1956). The quotation is from Hicks's *Journal*, 185.

7. The quotation is from Walt Whitman and is cited by Jones in *Later Periods*, I, 441.

8. Hicks, *Journal*, 315.

9. Quoted by Forbush, *Elias Hicks*, 192.

10. *Ibid.*, 280–281.

11. *Ibid.*, 144–150.

CHAPTER III

1. The following discussion of sect-church development is based on general reading in the sociology of religion rather than any specific work.

However, some works ought to be cited for their usefulness: Liston Pope, *Millhands and Preachers* (New Haven, Conn., 1942); J. Milton Yinger, *Religion, Society and the Individual* (New York, 1957); Bryan R. Wilson, "An Analysis of Sect Development," *American Sociological Review*, XXIV (February, 1959), 3–15; Benton Johnson, "A Critical Appraisal of Church-Sect Typology," *American Sociological Review*, XXII (February, 1957), 88–92; and Harold F. Pfautz, "The Sociology of Secularization," *American Journal of Sociology*, LXI (September, 1955), 121–28.

2. On alienation see: Melvin Seeman, "On the Meaning of Alienation," *American Sociological Review*, XXIV (December, 1959), 783–791.

3. Liston Pope, *Millhands and Preachers*. The changes listed in the table below are quoted from Pope, 122–124.

4. The following list does not include all the leaders and active participants in the Separation. Only those on whom data could be obtained are included. The term *real estate* refers to assessed value of property as found in the Philadelphia poor tax records. The term *estate* refers to the total value of property at death as revealed in wills. Data were accumulated from many sources: newspaper and magazine obituaries, Quaker memorials, general histories of the Society of Friends, and the Philadelphia city directories were especially helpful. Most of the data on wealth came from the poor tax records, MSS., Philadelphia City Archives, City Hall, Philadelphia, Pennsylvania and from private wills of the persons involved.

5. See Chapter VI.

6. Sociologists argue with considerable force that social mobility, not wealth or social status, is the primary source of anomie and alienation. They especially emphasize the importance of the rate of mobility as a key to understanding relative degrees of alienation. All this is perfectly true. An upwardly mobile individual may well experience feelings of uneasiness in his new position. However, the anxieties of the upwardly mobile are likely to be more concerned with problems of adaptation to social structure and norms than rejection of them. In an acquisitive society like early nineteenth century America, which emphasized openness, equality of opportunity, and competitiveness, low social status can be used as an indication of alienation. In a society of this kind, low social status or lack of mobility is tantamount to failure. An excellent discussion of anomie and alienation can be found in Robert K. Merton, *Social Theory and Social Structure* (Glencoe, Illinois, 1957), 131–194 My assumption here is that in an acquisitive society wealth is a reflection of secular success and power. Wealthy persons would, then, possess power and would be likely to believe that a world which had rewarded them was properly organized as to values and institutions. On the other

hand, persons of little wealth would be subject to feelings of powerlessness and would be more likely to have anxieties about social norms and institutions.

7. The chart is based on the real estate assessments for the Philadelphia city poor tax. No other general tax records are now in existence for this period.

8. Data are again based on poor tax records. The curve was obtained by plotting percentages of people who became Hicksite or Orthodox against wealth in real estate.

9. The curve was obtained by plotting percentages of people who became Hicksite or Orthodox against the zones in which they resided. Zones are coterminous with electoral wards. Zonal figures were obtained by dividing the total real estate assessment per ward by the total population per ward. The technique used here is based upon the conceptual scheme suggested in William A. Sullivan, "Did Labor Support Andrew Jackson?" *Political Science Quarterly*, LXII (December, 1947), 569–580.

10. Social status is a difficult concept to deal with, especially in a historical context. Participants in the Hicksite-Orthodox schism did express ideas about status. Therefore, it does seem justifiable to apply the concept to this particular case. The difficult problem is to assign status ranks. The system of ranking used here is based upon the author's impressions gathered from reading the literature of the period, especially the views of foreign travelers, and upon the schemes presented in such books as: Merle Curti, and others, *The Making of an American Community* (Stanford, California, 1959), 222–258 and Walter Hugins, *Jacksonian Democracy and the Working Class* (Stanford, California, 1960).

11. Data on occupations were derived from Robert DiSilver, *DiSilver's Directory and Stranger's Guide, 1824–1835*.

12. My assumption is that any artisan owning his own shop would have been a master and that any artisan owning both a shop and a dwelling house must have been well-to-do. This assumption is confirmed by poor tax payments and property holdings. Real estate holdings can be found in the Register of Deeds, MSS., Philadelphia City Archives, City Hall, Philadelphia, Pennsylvania.

13. Both the clothing and building trades were undergoing rapid change at the time (c. 1830). Tension was especially high among the journeymen in these trades. As a whole, the masters were not subject to problems of the same intensity. Labor conflict in Philadelphia at this time was primarily between journeyman and master. On this problem see John R. Commons, et al., *History of Labour in the United States*, I (New York, 1921), 88–107, 185–231. The figures above represent my

attempts to discriminate between journeymen and masters. Here again, I assumed that anyone owning his own shop would be a master.

14. The table is based upon a random sample of the members of Meetings in the Philadelphia area. Place of residence can be determined from *DiSilver's Directory and Stranger's Guide*.

15. Movement can be traced through the certificates of removal which appear in the various Monthly Meetings for business. The above table is based on Monthly Meetings in Philadelphia and its immediate vicinity. Microfilm copies of the minutes of Monthly Meetings can be found in the Friends Historical Library of Swarthmore College.

CHAPTER IV

1. M. Pennock to S. Vickers, January 10, 1822, MSS., Chester County Historical Society in West Chester, Pennsylvania (hereafter referred to as C.C.H.S.).

2. M. Pennock to Mary Jones, February, 1828, MSS., C.C.H.S.

3. The numerical split can be found in Jeremiah Foster, *An Authentic Report*, II (Philadelphia, 1831), 464. The best place to follow the course of the nonurban Separations is in the minutes of the various Monthly meetings, MSS., Friends Historical Library of Swarthmore College.

4. Frederick B. Tolles, *James Logan and the Culture of Provincial America* (Boston, 1957), 53.

5. On Chester and Delaware Counties see: Henry G. Ashmead, *History of Delaware County* (Philadelphia, 1884); John W. Jordan (ed.), *History of Delaware County Pennsylvania* (New York, 1914); and Gilbert Cope and J. S. Futhey, *History of Chester County Pennsylvania* (Philadelphia, 1881). See also the file of newspaper clippings maintained by the Chester County Historical Society.

6. Gilbert Cope, "A History of Agriculture in Chester County, Pennsylvania," MSS., C.C.H.S.; Stevenson N. Fletcher, *Pennsylvania Agriculture and Country Life* (Harrisburg, Pennsylvania, 1950), *passim*.

7. Samuel Bunting, "Journal," MSS., Friends Historical Library.

8. Fletcher, *Pennsylvania Agriculture*, 101–159, 222, 319.

9. *Ibid.*

10. Eli K. Price, *Memoir of Philip and Rachel Price* (Philadelphia, 1852); Jesse Kersey, *Narrative of the Early Life and Labors of Jesse Kersey* (Philadelphia, 1851).

11. Data on property, occupation, and ownership of cattle come from poor tax records for Chester County, 1827, MSS. C.C.H.S. and poor tax records for Delaware County, 1805–1810, MSS., Delaware County Historical Society in Chester, Pennsylvania. See appendix.

12. I do not intend to suggest that all farmers who owned more than three cattle were engaged in commercial agriculture or that any farmer who owned three or less was not. My object is only to compare the relative tendencies of Hicksite and Orthodox Friends to engage in commercial agriculture.

13. Data on mortgages come from the Mortgage Index for Chester County, MSS., in the Chester County Court House, West Chester, Pennsylvania and the Mortgage Index for Delaware County, MSS., in the Delaware County Court House, Media, Pennsylvania.

14. *American Republican and Anti-Masonic Register* (West Chester, Pennsylvania), January 12, 1825; William B. Evans, *Jonathan Evans* (Boston, 1959), 132–133.

15. William Lippincott, "Journal," MSS., Friends Historical Library.

16. Elias Hicks, *Journal* (New York, 1832), 185.

17. The numerical split of individual meetings can be found in their minutes and membership records. Meeting records and minutes are in the Friends Historical Library.

18. *A Brief History of the Westtown Boarding School* (Philadelphia, 1872).

19. For a general discussion of this phenomenon see Robert K. Merton, "Patterns of Influence: Local and Cosmopolitan Influentials," *Social Theory and Social Structure* (Glencoe, Illinois, 1957), 387–420.

CHAPTER V

1. Samuel Bettle to Jane Bettle, July 22, 1808. Jonathan Evans, Will, MSS., Quaker Collection of Haverford College. Thomas Stewardson, Will, MSS., Registry of Wills, City Hall, Philadelphia, Pennsylvania. See also the wills of Othniel Alsop, Samuel Bettle, Thomas P. and Henry Cope, Samuel P. Griffiths, Richard Humphreys, Isaac Lloyd, Caleb Pierce, Joseph Scattergood, Leonard Snowden, Thomas Wistar, and Ellis Yarnall. These wills are all in the Philadelphia Registry of Wills.

2. Stewardson Collection, Historical Society of Pennsylvania; Cope Collection, Quaker Collection.

3. *The Friend,* V (September 22, 1832), 398–400, and *passim.*

4. See the wills cited in footnote 1 above and memorials of Orthodox leaders in the Friends Historical Library.

5. I have traced the mobility of Orthodox leaders by comparing their wealth and occupation with those of their parents. Of those for whom data could be obtained twelve had risen in position, two had remained about the same and none had declined.

6. Jonathan Evans, "An Account of the Pine Street Meeting of 1819," MSS., Quaker Collection.

7. John Cockburn, *Cockburn's Review* (Philadelphia, 1829), 53–59. Benjamin Ferris, "A Historical Review of the Separation," 1–7, MSS., Friends Historical Library.

8. Here I am only guessing. I could find no direct statement which would confirm my impressions. This idea is, however, a common theme in Hicksite descriptions of the Separation.

9. E. Digby Baltzell discusses neighborhoods in Philadelphia in *An American Business Aristocracy* (New York, 1962), 199–251. Place of residence of Orthodox Friends can be traced through Robert DiSilver, *DiSilver's Directory and Stranger's Guide, 1824–1835.*

10. Personal, family and business ties are revealed in the correspondence of Orthodox Friends which can be found in the Quaker Collection.

11. Lists of visiting ministers may be found in the Quaker Collection of Haverford College. Orthodox attitudes toward England are revealed in their correspondence. See especially the Thomas Stewardson Collection in the Historical Society of Pennsylvania.

12. William Evans, *Journal* (Philadelphia, 1870), 16.

13. My impressions about the origins of Orthodoxy are based primarily on the correspondence of Jonathan Evans, MSS., Quaker Collection. The quotation is from Jonathan Evans to Richard Mott, April 29, 1802. Also revealing are the reactions of Orthodox Friends to the Hannah Bernard case in Ireland. See, for example, Richard Jordan, "Journal," *Friend's Library*, XIII (1849), 318. The "crisis theme" also appears in the correspondence of Samuel Bettle, William Evans, Thomas Evans, William Allinson, and Ellis Yarnall, MSS., Quaker Collection.

14. Jane Bettle, "An Account of the Separation, 1833," MSS., Quaker Collection. There do not appear to have been any direct connection between the New Light movement and the Hicksites. However, Friends in the Philadelphia area were aware of events in New England and saw them as analogous to the situation in Philadelphia Yearly Meeting.

15. [anonymous] to Samuel and Jane Bettle, January 8, 1826.

CHAPTER VI

1. These themes are expressed in such contemporary accounts of the Separation as: Benjamin Ferris, "A Historical Review of the Rise and Progress of the Separation," MSS., Friends Historical Library; Benjamin Ferris, "An Account of the Separation," MSS., Friends Historical Library; James Cockburn, *Cockburn's Review* (Philadelphia, 1829); Halliday Jackson, "A History of the Separation," MSS., Friends Historical

Library; *The Berean, A Religious Publication,* III (May, 1827), 322–323.

2. On egalitarianism see: Lee Benson, *The Concept of Jacksonian Democracy,* Atheneum edition (New York, 1964). Examples of Quaker use of egalitarian ideas can be found in: *Cockburn's Review,* 57; *Berean,* III (March 6, 1827), 241–242; III (May 1, 1827), 305; Edward Hicks, *Memoirs* (Philadelphia, 1851), 110; Benjamin Ferris, "An Account of the Separation," 1; and Thomas McClintock to William Poole, February, 1827, Ferris Papers.

3. Some understanding of the ferment in American religion can be gained from Alice F. Tyler, *Freedom's Ferment* (Minneapolis, Minnesota, 1944) and W. W. Sweet, *Religion in the Development of American Culture, 1765–1840* (New York, 1952). Also important is Whitney Cross, *The Burned-Over District* (Ithaca, New York, 1950).

4. Hicksite liberals were more interested in the Unitarian controversy than were the two other groups. The liberals saw the Unitarians as allies in the struggle against a broad-based Orthodox conspiracy. At least one of the liberals, Benjamin Ferris, had some understanding of the social and theological complexities of the situation in New England, but the majority of the liberals did not. They simply felt that the two movements had identical aims. Liberals felt a similar affinity for Thomas Jefferson because of his role in religious disestablishment in Virginia. See Benjamin Ferris, "An Account of the Separation," 70; *Berean,* I (February 1, 1825), 359, 362–366; I (February 23, 1824), 6–8; II (September 20, 1825), 98–102.

5. I have traced some of the effects of family on the Separation through a random sample of the characteristics of more than 1000 Friends. The best way to understand the complex relationship of the Hicksite leaders is to read their correspondence in the Ferris Papers, MSS., Friends Historical Library.

6. Samuel Comfort, "Journal," MSS., Friends Historical Library; Halliday Jackson, "A History of the Separation."

7. John Comly, *Journal* (Philadelphia, 1853).

8. James Mott to his parents, July 6, 1819, cited in Anna Davis Hallowell, *Life and Letters of James and Lucretia Mott* (Boston, 1884), 68.

9. The best expression of the Hicksite liberal viewpoint is in *The Berean,* I–IV (Wilmington, Delaware, 1824–1828).

10. On Benjamin Ferris see clipping of "Memorial Presented to the Historical Society of Delaware," *Papers of Delaware Historical Society for 1903* in the Friends Historical Library. Ferris's papers have been collected in the same library and are revealing. Also important is Jean

McClure, "Benjamin Ferris," typed manuscript which is also in the Friends Historical Library.

11. See, for example, *Berean,* II (September 20, 1825), 98–102; I (March 22, 1825), 399–400; and II (December 13, 1825), 187.

12. *Ibid.* and also *The Berean,* III (July 10, 1827), 385.

13. *The Berean,* I (April 20, 1824), 78–79; II (October 3, 1825), 97–98; II (October 17, 1825), 115; II (December 27, 1825), 195–196. Also important are: Thomas McClintock to William Poole, n.d., Ferris Papers; and *The Advocate of Truth,* I (March, 1828), 67.

14. The best and most sophisticated attack on Orthodox doctrine is in Benjamin Ferris and Eliphalet Gilbert, *The Letters of Paul and Amicus* (Philadelphia, 1823). Similar material is scattered throughout *The Berean.*

15. *The Berean,* II (March 7, 1826), 274; II (September 6, 1825), 69; III (May 15, 1827), 322–323.

16. References to Robert Owen are scattered through the 1825 and 1826 issues of *The Berean.* For example, see *The Berean,* II (November 15, 1825), 145–146; II (September 6, 1825), 168–169; II (January 24, 1826), 243. The neat tripartite division of the Hicksite movement into liberal, traditional, and sectarian is, in some respects, overly simple. The distinctions outlined here were blurred. Certainly no clear-cut separation can be established between traditional and sectarian factions. Despite its limitations the overall framework is both valid and useful. At least it suggests the main outlines of the complexities of the Hicksite movement.

17. It is interesting that the Hicksites seem to be expressing the same pattern of nostalgia and progress which characterized society at large. See Marvin Meyers, *Jacksonian Persuasion* (Stanford, California, 1959).

18. The best guides to the Hicksite consensus are the statements of protest written by Hicksites immediately following the Separation. Most of these statements can be found in *Cockburn's Review.* Also helpful are the minutes of the various Hicksite Meetings (1828–1832). Microfilm copies of these minutes can be found in the Friends Historical Library.

19. Minutes of Philadelphia Yearly Meeting (Hicksite), 1828–1832. Also William Poole to Benjamin Ferris, April 18, 1826, Ferris Papers; William Wharton to Elias Hicks, March 8, 1827, Ferris Papers; Thomas McClintock to William Poole, February, 1827, Ferris Papers; and *The Berean,* III (May 15, 1827), 324–326.

20. Minutes of Philadelphia Yearly Meeting (Hicksite), 1828–1832.

Appendixes

A. Comparison of Quakers and Non-Quakers

COMPARISON OF QUAKERS AND NON-QUAKERS IN PHILADELPHIA, PENNSYLVANIA

Wealth: Real Estate				
Assessed Value of Real Estate	QUAKER		NON-QUAKER	
	Number	Per cent	Number	Per cent
0	42	30	214	46
1–999	18	13	92	20
1000–1999	16	11	46	10
2000–2999	11	8	41	9
3000–3999	10	7	29	6
4000–	43	30	43	9
Total	140	99	465	100

Occupation	QUAKER		NON-QUAKER	
	Number	Per cent	Number	Per cent
Gentleman	49	13	5	2
Merchant-importer	47	12	9	3
Professional	23	6	9	3
Business-manufacturing	104	27	67	22
Semiprofessional	37	9	18	6
Artisan	127	33	192	64
Total	387	100	300	100

COMPARISON OF QUAKER AND NON-QUAKER FARMERS IN CHESTER COUNTY, PENNSYLVANIA

Number of cattle

Number of mature cattle	QUAKER		NON-QUAKER	
	Number	Per cent	Number	Per cent
1–3	90	52	420	67
4–5	36	21	147	24
6–	47	28	57	9
Total	173	101	624	100

Size of farms

Size of farm (in acres)	QUAKER		NON-QUAKER	
	Number	Per cent	Number	Per cent
1–49	25	15	165	26
50–99	49	29	201	32
100–149	50	29	161	26
150–199	24	14	60	10
200–	21	12	37	6
Total	169	99	624	100

Value of farms

Value of farm (in $)	QUAKER		NON-QUAKER	
	Number	Per cent	Number	Per cent
1–1999	41	21	191	31
2000–3999	58	30	222	36
4000–5999	43	22	127	20
6000–7999	19	10	36	6
8000–	35	18	48	8
Total	196	101	624	101

B. Orthodox Quakers in Philadelphia

ORTHODOX

Name	Occupation	Residence	Ward	Wealth (real estate in $)
Timothy Abbott	Currier	17 S. 3rd	Walnut	5,000
Charles Allen	Druggist	180 S. 2nd	Pine	?
Sarah Allipone	?	139 Walnut	Walnut	?
Caleb Ash	Apothecary	66 N. 9th	Walnut or Pine	?
Joshua Ash	Dealer	29 N. 4th	L. Delaware	?
Marshall Attmore	Watchmaker	7 Church Alley	High	0
George V. Bacon	Accountant	283 Filbert	North	?
Elizabeth Baker	Gentlewoman (widow)	58 Mulberry	High	2,250
Hannah Baker	?	72 N. 5th	L. Delaware	2,000
Rebecca Barnes	Gentlewoman	165 Walnut	South	?
Isaac Barton	Merchant	30 S. 2nd	Chestnut	?
Elizabeth Bates	Nurse	450 S. Front	Southwark	?
Ann Bedford	?	81 S. 3rd	Dock	?
Edward Bettle	?	14 S. 3rd	Chestnut	?
Samuel Bettle	Clothing merchant	14 S. 3rd	Chestnut	12,000

ORTHODOX (Continued)

Name	Occupation	Residence	Ward	Wealth (real estate in $)
Thomas Bettle	?	40 N. 5th	High	?
Thomas Bickham	Gentleman	254 S. Front	Southwark	?
William Biddle	Druggist	4th and Race	L. Delaware	3,100
Jeremiah Boone	Merchant	163 Pine	Pine	?
Thomas Booth	Accountant	144 Sassafras	L. Delaware	?
Samuel D. Breed	Shoe store	6 N. 6th	High	0
David S. Brown	?	4th and Browne	N. Liberties	?
Jeremiah Brown	?	383 Mulberry	S. Mulberry	510
Moses Brown	Merchant	6th and Mulberry	High	2,600
William Brown	Printer	6 John	N. Liberties	?
William Buckley	Gentleman	87 S. 3rd	Dock	11,000
Nathan Bunker	Flour merchant	22 Washington Sq.	Dock	2,500
Elizabeth Burns	Gentlewoman	152 Locust	Locust	0
William H. Burr	?	200 Mulberry	North	2,500
John Burson	Commission merchant	171 S. 3rd	New Market	1,200
Amos W. Butcher	Grocer and agent for N.Y. packets	49 N. Water	High	3,450
Francis Campion	Accountant	25 N. 5th	L. Delaware	?
Caleb Canby	Plumber	137 High	High	?
Merritt Canby	?	4th and Prune	Dock	1,500

Name	Occupation	Address	District	Value
William Chambers	?	31 Cedar	New Market	0
Mordecai Churchman	?	190 Pine	New Market	1,680
Joseph Clark	Gentleman	24 N. 6th	High	?
Samuel Clement	?	184 Market	Chestnut	?
George M. Coates	China merchant	49 High	High	8,650
John Coates	Sailmaker	60 Plum	Southwark	?
Samuel Coates	Junior accountant	210 S. 4th	Southwark	?
Solomon W. Conrad	Printer	39 Zane	North	?
John Cooper	Printer	10 Green's Ct.	Pine	0
Israel Cope	Gentleman	86 Mulberry	North	5,250
Thomas P. Cope	Merchant	36 N. 4th	High	48,000
Zaccheus Collins	Gentleman	29 N. 2nd	High	7,000
Elizabeth Corbit	Grocer	Queen & Front	N. Liberties	?
Joseph Corlies	?	Dean below Locust	Locust	1,000
Wm. Cowperthwaite	Dry goods merchant	95 S. 8th	Locust	4,000
Elizabeth Cox	Gentlewoman	Union and 3rd	Dock	?
Mary Cox	Teacher	234 Sassafras	L. Delaware	0
Sarah A. Cox	Shopkeeper	120 Filbert	North	?
John Cozins	Drayman	166 St. John	N. Liberties	?
Benjamin Cresson	China merchant	197 Sassafras	U. Delaware	2,500
John H. Cresson	China merchant	37 N. 7th	High	?
Joseph Cruikshank	Gentleman	16 & 20 Church Alley	High	?
John Culin	Tailor	25 Water	High	?

ORTHODOX (Continued)

Name	Occupation	Residence	Ward	Wealth (real estate in $)
Margaret Curtis	16 Combs Alley	Mangler	High	?
David P. Davis	72 N. 9th	?	S. Mulberry	0
Elizabeth Davis	42 N. 4th	Dry goods store	L. Delaware	0
Isaac R. Davis	134 S. 4th	Shopkeeper	Pine	0
Mary Davis	Chestnut W. of Broad	Seamstress	Middle	0
Mordecai Dawson	77 Chestnut	Brewer	Chestnut	14,350
Hannah Dillin	102 N. 9th	Dry goods store	N. or S. Mulberry	?
George M. Elkinton	202 N. 2nd	Chandler	N. Liberties	?
Joseph Ely	188 Mulberry	Flour merchant	North	7,100
Goveyneer Emerson	51 S. 5th	Physician	Dock	?
Samuel Emlen	247 Mulberry	Physician	S. Mulberry	11,000
Charles Evans	270 Mulberry	Druggist	North	?
Sarah Evans	60 N. 8th	?	S. Mulberry	?
Jonathan Fell	52 S. Front	Chocolate and mustard manufacturer	Walnut	?
Redwood Fisher	116 Mulberry	?	High	5,700
Charles F. Folwell	90 N. Front	Gentleman	L. Delaware	?
Thomas Folwell	118 Chestnut	Dry goods merchant	Walnut	?
William Folwell	233 Mulberry	Dry goods merchant	L. Delaware	6,000

Name	Occupation	Address	Location	Value
William Foster	Merchant	111 Mulberry	L. Delaware	?
James H. Gardiner	Grocer	145 S. 8th	Cedar	?
John K. Garrett	Bottler	19 N. Alley	?	?
Philip Garrett	Watchmaker	9 N. 6th	High	o
Samuel P. Garrigues	Constable	239 Mulberry	L. Delaware	o
Joseph Gibbons	Conveyancer	149 S. 10th	Cedar	?
Mahlon Gillingham	Auctioneer	172 Mulberry	North	?
William Govett	Gentleman	244 Filbert	North	?
James R. Greeves	Carpenter	47 S. 10th	South	5,500
Isaiah Hacker	Merchant	190 Mulberry	North	?
Joseph Hackney, Jr.	?	6 Hartung's Alley	High	?
John Hallowell	Judge	Near Girard College	Penn Township	?
Joshua Harlan	Merchant	72 S. 3rd	Walnut	?
Pattison Hartshorn	Gentleman	304 Mulberry	North	?
Joseph Hartshorne	Physician	272 Mulberry	North	6,800
Mary Hayes	Shopkeeper	21 N. 9th	North	?
Mary Hillman	Teacher	43 Vine	?	?
Abraham Hilyard	?	10 N. 6th	High	?
Samuel Holgate	Shoemaker	389 S. Front	Southwark	?
Robert Hopkins	Dry goods store	182 S. 2nd	Pine	?
Benjamin Hornor	Gentleman	62 N. 3rd	L. Delaware	?
John Horton	Bricklayer	20 Greenleaf's Ct.	Chestnut	?
Sarah Howard	Washwoman	122 Lombard	New Market or Cedar	?

ORTHODOX (Continued)

Name	Occupation	Residence	Ward	Wealth (real estate in $)
Edward W. Howell	Gentleman	12 Prune	Dock	?
Israel Howell	Currier	150 S. 9th	Cedar	?
John B. Howell	Botanic physician	17 N. 6th	L. Delaware	1,040
Joseph Howell	Leather merchant	217 Spruce	Locust	7,500
Richard V. Humphreys	?	32 Swanson	Southwark	?
Joseph James	Gentleman	171 Pine	Pine	?
Thomas James	Medical school professor	7 York Buildings	?	?
Halliday Jenkins	Trader	202 N. 2nd	N. Liberties	?
Joseph Jenkins	Trader	7 Letitia Ct.	Chestnut	?
Joseph R. Jenks	Flour merchant	5 Vine	?	?
Ruth Jess	Bonnetmaker	1 Church Alley	High	0
Samuel Jobson	Glue manufacturer	273 N. 3rd	N. Liberties	?
Joseph Johnson	Ship chandler	184 Chestnut	South	1,200
Sarah Johnson	?	176 Mulberry	North	?
George D. Jones	Cabinetmaker	2 Library	Walnut	?
Isaac C. Jones	Importer	263 Mulberry	S. Mulberry	5,500
Jeremiah Jones	Shoemaker	534 S. Front	Southwark	?

Samuel W. Jones	Merchant	154 N. Front	U. Delaware	3,500
William Jones	Commission merchant	325 Mulberry	S. Mulberry	180
Thomas Kimber	Bookseller	216 Mulberry	North	3,000
Benjamin Kite	Bookseller	20 N. 3rd	High	?
Thomas Kite	Bookseller	137 High	High	0
Samuel Knight	Importer	202 Mulberry	North	0 ?
James Large	Merchant	298 Mulberry	North	1,520
John R. Latimer	Merchant	4th and Prune	North	?
John Leedom	Iron merchant	29 Pine	Dock	5,000
John Letchworth	China store	50 N. Front	Pine	0
Ebenezer Levick	Currier, leather store	2nd & Callowhill	High	
Elizabeth Lewis	Gentlewoman	260 S. Front	N. Liberties	?
Mordecai Lewis	Merchant	283 Spruce	Southwark	?
Samuel N. Lewis	?	232 Walnut	Locust ?	?
Samuel Lippincott	Cabinetmaker	5 Callowhill	Locust	?
Margaret Lisle	Gentlewoman	127 S. 2nd	N. Liberties	?
John Livezy	?	50 N. Water	Dock	?
Isaac S. Lloyd	Merchant	87 High	High	800
Joshua Longstreth	Merchant	185 Mulberry	High	67,000
Edward Lownes	Silversmith	142 Chestnut	L. Delaware	20,700
Chillion Lukens	Cabinetmaker	270 South	Walnut	?
John McCollin	Accountant	125 S. 3rd	?	?
Benjamin Marshall	Accountant	170 S. 11th	?	?

ORTHODOX (Continued)

Name	Occupation	Residence	Ward	Wealth (real estate in $)
Charles Marshall	Druggist	221 High	High	1,000
William Master	Ladies shoemaker	145 Vine	?	?
Caleb Maule	Lumber merchant	90 Vine	?	?
William Maule	Lumber merchant	198 N. 4th	N. Liberties	?
Lloyd Mifflin	Gentleman	252 Spruce	Locust	4,000
Rachel Miller	Dry goods store	34 N. 2nd	High	?
William Molands	Physician	72 Locust	?	?
Catharine Morris	Gentlewoman	56 N. 4th	L. Delaware	1,050
William Morrison	Brewer	132 S. 3rd	Southwark (?)	?
Edward Needles, Sr.	Druggist	12th & Sassafras	N. Mulberry	?
John Needles, Jr.	Wireworker	130 N. Front	U. Delaware	1,100
Michael Newbold	Grazier	77 S. 6th	?	?
Thomas Parke	Physician	1 Rittenhouse Pl.	Locust	?
Beulah Parker	?	137 Mulberry	L. Delaware	?
David Parry	Flour store	?	?	?
Robert Pearsall, Jr.	Druggist	4 N. 11th	?	?
Caleb Peirce	Hardware merchant	10 Church Alley	High	3,000
John Peirson	Tanner	445 N. Front	?	?
Elliston Perot	Importer	299 High	North	16,300
William S. Perot	Brewer	120 Vine	U. Delaware	200

Name	Occupation	Address	District	Value
Charles Pleasants	Gentleman	5 S. 11th	?	?
Joseph K. Potts	Merchant	1 Mulberry Ct.	High	?
Joseph Price	Upholsterer	61 Race	U. Delaware	1,750
George F. Randolph	Merchant	182 Mulberry	North	0 ?
Samuel B. Rawle	Merchant	112 S. 3rd	?	?
William Redwood	Gentleman	98 S. 3rd	?	?
Isaac Reeve	Carpenter	Torr's Court	N. Liberties	?
Clement Remington	Gentleman	192 N. 6th	N. Liberties	?
Job B. Remington	Merchant	334 Mulberry	North	?
Sarah A. Remington	Storekeeper	308 S. 2nd	?	?
John Richards	Printer	20 Church Alley	High	7,360
John Ridgway	Bricklayer	76 N. 9th	?	?
Charles Roberts	Gentleman	174 Mulberry	North	3,100
Joseph Roberts, Jr.	Teacher	2 Library	Walnut	1,800
George Robinson	Currier	206 N. 4th	N. Liberties	?
Thomas Rogers	Brass founder	61 Mulberry	L. Delaware	?
William Sansom	Gentleman	96 Mulberry	High	5,250
William Savery	Lumber merchant	20 N. 5th	High	4,000
James Sellers	Wireworker	12th and High	?	?
John Sharp	Merchant	154 S. 9th	?	?
Joseph Sharp	Dry goods store	9 S. 2nd	?	?
Blakely Sharpless	Bookseller	178 S. Front	?	?
Townsend Sharpless	Dry goods store	30 S. 2nd	?	?
Earl Shinn	Bricklayer	29 Elizabeth	?	?

ORTHODOX (Continued)

Name	Occupation	Residence	Ward	Wealth (real estate in $)
Samuel Shinn	Bricklayer	134 Pine	Pine	4,600
Thomas Shipley	Hardware merchant	202 Mulberry	North	?
Jacob Shoemaker	Paper hanging warehouse	27 N. 12th	North	?
Edward Simmons, Jr.	Merchant	85 Wood	N. Liberties	?
William Simmons	Weighmaster	77 Tammany	?	?
James Sleeper	Stove factory	24 Elfreth's Alley	L. Delaware	725
Nehemiah Sleeper	Umbrella manufac- turer	45 N. 2nd	High	?
Benjamin Smith	Accountant	277 Walnut	South	?
Charles W. Smith	Merchant	251 Mulberry	S. Mulberry	4,850
Daniel B. Smith	Druggist	45 N. 6th	High	2,900
Jacob R. Smith	Dentist	99 S. 5th	?	?
John J. Smith, Jr.	Newspaper editor	135 Mulberry	L. Delaware	6,700
Morris Smith	Merchant	319 Sassafras	N. Mulberry	?
Richard Smith	Bookseller	42 N. 2nd	High	?
Seth Smith	Teacher	98 Mulberry	High	?
Stephen Smith	Wool merchant	174 S. Front	?	?
Leonard Snowden	China merchant	242 N. 3rd	N. Liberties	?
Rebecca Snowden	Gentlewoman	106 S. Front	?	?

Name	Occupation	Address	Street	Amount
Robert Steel	Silverplater	223 Callowhill	?	?
Robert Steele	Gentleman	257 Spruce	Locust	?
George Stewardson	?	92 Mulberry	High	0
Thomas Stewardson	Gentleman	90 Mulberry	High	22,600
John Stokes	Merchant	10 John	?	?
Charles Stow	Dry goods store	38 N. 6th	High	?
Thomas Stroud	Merchant	10 N. 6th	High	?
Isaac P. Taylor	Teacher	3 Carleton Sq.	?	?
Francis Thompson, Jr.	Merchant	164 Mulberry	High	?
Jesse Thomson	Physician	2 Thomson's Ct.	?	?
Samuel F. Troth	Druggist	222 High	Chestnut	?
Thomas S. Tucker	Tailor	2 S. 8th	?	?
Benjamin Valentine	Agent	154 Mulberry	High	0
George Vaux	Lawyer	145 Mulberry	L. Delaware	5,100
Robert Vaux	Gentleman	346 Mulberry	North	2,800
Lewis Walker	Hatter	358 High	Middle	?
William M. Walmsley	Broker	98 S. 4th	?	?
Joseph Walton	Bookseller	43 N. Front	High	?
Benjamin Warder	Merchant	179 Vine	?	?
William S. Warder	Merchant	117 Sassafras	U. Delaware	950
Jesse Waterman	Tea warehouse	88 S. 5th	?	?
John Webster	Liquor store	425 High	North	?
Thomas C. Wharton	Broker	87 Pine	Pine	2,250

ORTHODOX (Continued)

Name	Occupation	Residence	Ward	Wealth (real estate in $)
Margaret Wharton	Gentlewoman	242 Walnut	Dock	?
Josiah White	Gentleman	128 Mulberry	High	11,000
Richard Williams	Dry goods merchant	14 Church Alley	?	?
Jesse Williamson	Sailmaker	92 N. Water	L. Delaware	?
Susanna Willis	Shopkeeper	S. 13th & Walnut	?	?
Joseph B. Willits	Bricklayer	?	?	?
James Winter	Band box maker	157 N. 2nd	U. Delaware	0
Bartholomew Wistar	Merchant	255 Mulberry	S. Mulberry	9,050
Elizabeth Wistar	Gentlewoman	Washington Square	Dock	2,000
Thomas Wistar	Gentleman	383 High	North	14,700
Richard C. Wood	Lawyer	70 S. 4th	Walnut	?
Richard D. Wood	Druggist	65 Mulberry	L. Delaware	5,100
Samuel C. Wood	Merchant	72 S. High	Walnut	?
William A. Yardley	Merchant	142 S. 2nd	Dock	?
Ellis Yarnall	Gentleman	22 S. 12th	?	10,500

C. Hicksite Quakers in Philadelphia

HICKSITES

Name	Occupation	Residence	Ward	Wealth (real estate in $)
William S. Abbott	Brewer	71 Spruce	Dock	4,000
Enoch Allen	Tailor	15 Coomb's Alley	High	?
Jedediah Allen	Gentleman	76 S. 11th	Walnut or Pine	5,500
Sarah Ashbridge	Gentlewoman	48 Madison	N. Mulberry	?
Nathan Atherton, Jr.	Watchmaker	174 S. 11th	?	?
James P. Atkinson	Livery stable	99 Poplar Lane	N. Liberties	?
Joel Atkinson	?	Cherry W. of 10th	S. Mulberry	4,850
Samuel C. Atkinson	Editor	9 Branch	U. Delaware	60
Edwin P. Atlee	Physician	122 N. 5th	U. Delaware	?
Nathan Baily	Merchant	14 Juliana	?	?
Joshua Bailey, Jr.	Merchant	5 Church Alley	High	0
Newsom Baker	Carpenter	187 Green	Pine	?
George Baker	Founder	109 Bud	Pine	?
Jacob Ballenger	Carpenter	70 N. 9th	S. Mulberry	9,100
Mark Baner	Porter	109 St. John	?	?
Thomas Barnes	Lamp store	26 S. 4th	Chestnut	4,000

HICKSITES (Continued)

Name	Occupation	Residence	Ward	Wealth (real estate in $)
Titus Bennett	Bookseller	37 High	High	7,780
Richard K. Betts	Carpenter	Sch. 8th & Ann	North	600
Clement Biddle	Sugar refiner	164 Mulberry	North	3,400
Elizabeth Biddle	Gentlewoman	142 High	Chestnut	?
James Boustead	Currier	12 Emlen Ct.	?	?
John Bouvier	Lawyer	Filbert & 12th	North	?
Joseph Brick	Porter	Juliana	?	?
Benjamin Brown	Printer	139 Lombard	New Market	?
Alice Bunting	Teacher	117 N. Front	L. Delaware	0
Joseph Burr	Painter	225 Lombard	New Market	220
William Burton	Physician	199 S. 4th	?	?
Frances W. Buzby	Dry goods store	268 N. Second	N. Liberties	?
William N. Buzby	Painter	19 Pine Alley	Southwark	?
Stephen Byerly	Merchant	22 New	U. Delaware	?
Jonathan Carmalt	Conveyancer	302 N. 3rd	N. Liberties	?
Sharon Carter	Agent for Jersey Glass Co.	281 High	North	1,200
Charles Champion	Innkeeper	1 Mulberry	L. Delaware	0
Thomas Chandler	?	92 N. 4th	L. Delaware	?
Josiah Chapman	?	18 Branch	U. Delaware	0

Name	Occupation	Address	Area	
Caleb Coates	?	N. 9th & Cherry	U. Delaware	0
James Cockburn	Manufacturer	George and 13th	?	?
George Coffee	Sprig cutter	16 German	?	?
Thomas M. Coffin	Merchant	3 Mulberry	L. Delaware	?
John G. Cole	Tailor	28 Tammany	?	?
Lydia Comfort	?	191 Mulberry	L. Delaware	?
James Conway	Blacksmith	61 Apple	N. Liberties	0
Samuel C. Cooper	Tailor	5 Chancery La.	High	0
Joseph Corbit	Sugar refiner	228 Mulberry	North	?
Jacob W. Corlies	Merchant	160 Mulberry	North	?
Joseph Cowperth-waite	Cashier	82 Dillwyn Ct.	?	?
David H. Davis	Merchant	72 Vine	U. Delaware	?
Samuel Dobson	?	115 Walnut	Walnut	?
Isaac Donaldson	China merchant	76 N. 2nd	L. Delaware	?
Benedict Dorsey	China store	132 N. 2nd	U. Delaware	40
Hannah Earl	?	249 High	High	0
Thomas Earle	Lawyer	199 N. 6th	N. Liberties	?
John C. Evans	Lumber merchant	145 N. 6th	N. Liberties	?
Joseph Evans	Shoemaker	Old York Road	?	?
William Eyre	Carpenter	Loxley's Ct.	Pine	800
Mary Field	Shopkeeper	284 N. 2nd	N. Liberties	?
Thomas S. Field	Farmer(?)	132 N. 2nd	U. Delaware	0
Preston Firth	Carpenter	28 Ann	Locust	?

HICKSITES (Continued)

Name	Occupation	Residence	Ward	Wealth (real estate in $)
Aaron Fogg	Bricklayer	12th N. of Arch	North	?
William Folwell, Jr.	Dry goods merchant	22 Mulberry	High	4,000
Richard P. Foulke	Grocer	24 S. 8th	Middle	?
William H. French	Plasterer	Morgan	Middle	?
Eliakim Garretson	Dry goods store	159 Vine	?	?
Edward B. Garrigues	Druggist	High and 6th	High	6,750
Abraham Garrigues	Agent	79 Mulberry	L. Delaware	0
William A. Garrigues	Teacher	37 Cherry	S. Mulberry	4,100
Clayton Gaskill	Carpenter	62 Cherry	L. Delaware	0
Joseph Gatchell	Blacksmith	57 N. 9th	S. Mulberry	1,900
John Gest	Flour merchant	28 N. 10th	North	?
George Gibbons	Conveyancer	151 N. 10th	?	?
William H. Gillingham	Physician	45 N. 8th	?	?
Henry D. Gilpin	District attorney	99 Walnut	Walnut	?
Sarah Griffin	?	31 Mulberry	L. Delaware	?
John D. Griscom	Physician	103 N. 5th	U. Delaware	?
Morris L. Hallowell	Commission merchant	38 N. Front	High	?
Jacob Hamer	Tailor	38 N. 6th	High	?
Samuel Hancock	Corder	33 N. Sch. 8th	North	?

Name	Occupation	Address	Location	
William Hancock	Shopkeeper	36 N. 2nd	High	?
Jeremiah Hartley	Watchmaker	139 Wood	?	?
Samuel Haydock	Plumber	4 Lodge	?	?
James Howell	Storekeeper	449 N. 2nd	N. Liberties	?
Hannah G. Hughes	Grocer	Frankford Rd.	?	?
Thomas J. Husband	Pharmacist	10th and Castle	N. Mulberry	?
John Hustler	Commission merchant	244 N. 3rd	N. Liberties	?
Samuel Hutchinson	Watchmaker	198 High	Chestnut	?
Richard Jackson	Tailor	50 N. 5th	High	?
William Johns	Painter	12th and Filbert	North	1,150
Josiah Johnson	Letter carrier	22 Little George	Walnut	0
George Justice	Hardware merchant	213 N. 4th	N. Liberties	?
Charles Keyser	Teacher	28 Palmyra Row	?	?
Jonathan Knight	Gentleman	305 N. 2nd	N. Liberties	?
David Knowles	Carpenter	82 Crown	U. Delaware	?
Samuel Konigmacher	Hardware merchant	104 Mulberry	High	?
Elijah Lawes, Sr.	Bedding merchant	312 High	Middle	0
Joseph Lea	Merchant	100 S. Front	Dock	?
Job Lewis	Cooper	43 New	U. Delaware	?
William Lindsay	Gentleman	117 N. 7th	N. Liberties	?
Elizabeth Lippincott	Milliner	179 N. 2nd	U. Delaware	?
Joshua Lippincott	Auctioneer	9 Clinton Sq.	Middle	?
Isaac Lippincott	Accountant	9 Kunckle	?	?

HICKSITES (Continued)

Name	Occupation	Residence	Ward	Wealth (real estate in $)
Charles Longstreth	Paper and hardware merchant	3 Church Alley	High	15
Joseph Lovering	Smith	2 S. 2nd	Dock	?
Benjamin Low	Teacher	14 Fromberg's Ct.	High	?
Elizabeth Lukens	Milliner	78 Mulberry	High	2,106
Samuel Marot	Cabinetmaker	437 N. 3rd	N. Liberties	?
William Marriott	Druggist	Mulberry & 5th	L. Delaware	?
Mary Ann Marshall	Milliner	175 S. 3rd	?	?
Robert V. Massey	Currier	245 N. 3rd	N. Liberties	?
John Mather, Jr.	Carpenter	6 Howard's Ct.	?	?
Philip Mendenhall	Accountant	90 N. Front	L. Delaware	0
Sarah Merritt	Milliner	67 Mulberry	L. Delaware	?
Enoch Middleton	Bricklayer	78 Dillwyn	?	?
Joseph Middleton	Gentleman	147 Mulberry	L. Delaware	2,600
Mary Middleton	Widow	3 Mustin's Ct.	N. Mulberry	?
Alexander Miller	Tailor	Diamond Ct.	South	?
Daniel Miller	Gentleman	Brown	N. Liberties	?
John Moore	Physician	214 Mulberry	North	?
James Mott	Commission merchant	14 Sansom	South	?
Samuel Newbold	Gentleman	18 Pine	Pine	?

Name	Occupation	Address	Ward	Amount
Jonathan Palmer	Teacher	193 Pine	Pine	4,400
Joshua Parke	Gentleman	141 Mulberry	L. Delaware	?
Joseph Parker	Justice of the peace	86 Wood	?	?
Thomas Parker, Jr.	Dry goods merchant	28 S. 2nd	?	?
Joseph Parrish	Physician	109 Mulberry	L. Delaware	5,700
Elizabeth Parvin	Teacher	117 N. 5th	N. Liberties	?
Richard Paxson	Hardware merchant	323 Mulberry	S. Mulberry	0
Nathaniel Pettit	Dry goods merchant	103 N. 2nd	L. Delaware	2,450
Mary Phipps	Gentlewoman	139 Dillwyn	?	?
Abigail Physick	Gentlewoman	210 N. 4th	N. Liberties	?
Samuel Pine	Carter	Type Alley	?	?
Jonas Preston	Physician	250 Mulberry	North	10,000
Eli K. Price	Lawyer	114 Mulberry	High	?
Richard Price	Merchant	46 N. 5th	L. Delaware	0
Joseph Pryor	Clerk of board of health	26 Elfreth's Alley	L. Delaware	675
John Rakestraw	Tailor	279 S. Front	?	?
David K. Reeder	Carpenter	Juliana	?	?
Charles Reeves	Hardware merchant	141 Arch	L. Delaware	?
Joseph Rhoads	Cabinetmaker	479 Sassafras	N. Mulberry	?
Samuel Richards	Iron merchant	347 Mulberry	S. Mulberry	3,550
Joseph Ridgeway	Tailor	10 S. 3rd	?	?
Thomas Ridgeway	Flour merchant	52 Vine	U. Delaware	55,000
Henry W. Ridgeway	Tailor	188 Cherry	?	?

HICKSITES (Continued)

Name	Occupation	Residence	Ward	Wealth (real estate in $)
Hugh Roberts	?	65 S. 11th	?	5,000
James Rowland, Jr.	Iron store	14 Frombs Ct.	?	?
John Rowlett	Author	47 Old York Rd.	?	?
John W. Rulon	Supercargo	19 New	U. Delaware	0
Joseph Sharpless	Dry goods merchant	14 S. 2nd	?	?
Alexander Shaw	Minter	St. Joseph's Ave.	Middle	?
John Sheppard	Victualler	James	?	?
Mark Sheppard	Blacksmith	Boy's Ct.	?	?
Caleb Shreve	Merchant	20 N. Front	High	?
Mordecai Simmons	Teacher	172 N. Front	N. Liberties	?
Jonathan Sleeper	China store	283 Sassafras	?	?
John Sleeper	Commission merchant	121 N. 2nd	L. Delaware	4,800
Josiah Smith	Accountant	76 Lombard	New Market	?
Samuel Smith	Teacher	N. 4th & Callowhill	N. Liberties	?
Samuel C. Spackman	Brickmaker	Callowhill c. 11th	N. Liberties	?
Sylvania Stokes	Milliner	6 Strawberry	Chestnut	?
Peter Thomas	Merchant	4 S. 2nd	?	?
Zebulon Thomas	Stable keeper	14 S. 2nd	?	?
William Thorne	Bricklayer	Truxton	Cedar	700
Joseph Trotter	Accountant	215 N. 4th	N. Liberties	?

Name	Occupation	Address	Street	Value
Joseph Truman	?	15 N. 7th	High	4,000
Benjamin Tucker	?	44 N. 5th	High	7,500
Thomas B. Vandevier	Gilder	115 N. 3rd	U. Delaware	?
Jane Vernon	Boardinghouse	55 Pine	Pine	?
William J. Wainwright	Grocer	81 N. Front	L. Delaware	2,250
Sarah Walker	Clothing store	6 Franklin Pl.	Walnut	?
Elwood Walter	Bookseller	145 N. 5th	N. Liberties	?
John Ward	Lottery broker	Powell and 6th	Pine	?
William Wayne	Hardware merchant	257 High	High	0
Rebecca Webb	Gentlewoman	140 Dillwyn	?	?
Reubon Webb	Currier	78 N. 4th	L. Delaware	50
William Wharton	Gentleman	?	?	2,600
Samuel White	Tailor	1 S. 13th	?	700
George Widdefield	Carpenter	171 High	?	?
James Widdefield	Carpenter	97 S. 8th	?	?
Peter Widdows	Teacher	4 Strawberry	Chestnut	0
Charles Williams	Lumber merchant	211 Walnut	South	400
John H. Willitts	Bricklayer	29 Palmyra Sq.	?	?
Nathan Wright	Carpenter	76 Green	?	?
Sarah Wright	Bonnet maker	15 N. 4th	High	?
William Yardley	Gentleman	125 Wood	Dock	6,500
Edmund Yeates	Tinplate worker	166 S. 6th	?	?

D. Orthodox Quakers in Delaware County

ORTHODOX

Name	Occupation	Size of Property (in acres)	Total Value of Property (in $)	Number of Cattle	Mortgage (size in $ and years in effect)
Nathan Garrett	Farmer	195	3,800	9	None
Thomas Garrett	Miller	315	6,465	4	None
William Garrett	Farmer	100	3,130	2	None
James Gorman	Farmer	149	2,250	4	None
Joseph Griffith	Farmer	75	1,275	3	None
Thomas Griffith	Farmer-tanner	98	3,020	5	None
David Hall	Farmer	108	3,365	5	None
James Hatton	Farmer	52	850	3	None
Jonathan Heacock	Farmer-grazier	112	3,660	10	None
Joseph Hibberd	Carpenter	54	1,060	3	None
Isaac Larkin	Farmer	197	2,020	3	None
Joseph Larkin	Farmer	121	1,520	2	None
Samuel Lewis	Miller	150	5,850	3	None
John Lewis	Miller	28	3,450	2	1,000; 1821–1822

Name	Occupation				
Richard Lloyd	Miller	27	6,100	3	None
Isaac Lobb	Farmer	90	1,820	7	None
John M. Maris	Farmer	50	1,650	4	None
William Maris	Farmer	80	1,170	0	None
George Martin	Farmer	95	2,560	2	None
John Morgan	Farmer	160	3,280	7	None
Joseph Newlin	Farmer	149	1,950	2	None
Nathan Newlin	Farmer	131	5,185	9	None
Joseph Palmer	Farmer-saddler	95	765	3	None
Moses Palmer	Farmer-grazier	167	3,710	12	None
Samuel Pancoast	Farmer	110	3,460	5	2,000; 1823–1833
Abraham & Joseph Pennell	Farmer-miller	280	8,355	15	3,200; 1813–1829
James Pennell	Farmer	80	1,695	1	1,725; ?–1828
Gillead Pennington	Farmer	30	320	2	None
Joseph Pyle	?	?	?	?	800; ?–1818
Joseph Rhoads	Farmer-tanner	178	5,600	7	None
Owen Rhoads	Farmer	230	7,070	10	None
Thomas Rudolph	?	?	?	?	5,300; 1820–
John Sellers	Farmer-tanner	100	2,130	11	None
Abraham Sharpless	Miller	24	4,875	5	None
William Sharpless	Farmer	40	2,200	2	None
William Smedley	Farmer	200	3,590	7	None
Joseph Talbot	Miller	100	2,280	3	None

ORTHODOX (Continued)

Name	Occupation	Size of Property (in acres)	Total Value of Property (in $)	Number of Cattle	Mortgage (size in $ and years in effect)
Samuel Trimble	Farmer	75	2,040	1	None
Isaac Yarnall	Farmer	170	2,905	5	1,600; ?–1831
James Yarnall	Farmer	250	4,470	8	None
William Yarnall (Edgemont)	Farmer	93	1,880	5	None
William Yarnall (Thornbury)	Farmer	170	4,725	10	None

E. Hicksite Quakers in Delaware County

HICKSITES

Name	Occupation	Size of Property (in acres)	Total Value of Property (in $)	Number of Cattle	Mortgage (size in $ and years in effect)
Cyrus Baker	Farmer	12	300	0	None
Benjamin Bartram	Farmer	114	3,700	9	None
John Bartram	Farmer	114	3,475	3	None
Joseph Bishop	Farmer	155	2,750	8	None
James Bonsall	Grist miller	2	1,075	1	None
Daniel Broomall	?	?	?	?	400; 1821–1825
James Broomall	Farmer	120	4,050	4	None
Thomas Broomall	Farmer(?)	?	50	1	None
Samuel Bunting	Farmer(?)	?	400	1	550; 1822–1824
Jesse Darlington	Farmer	171	5,050	12	1,200; 1798–1813
Samuel Davis	Farmer	116	2,335	3	None
William Davis	Farmer-wheelwright	100	1,880	5	None
William S. Davis	Farmer	32	1,280	1	None

HICKSITES (Continued)

Name	Occupation	Size of Property (in acres)	Total Value of Property (in $)	Number of Cattle	Mortgage (size in $ and years in effect)
Frederick Dicks	Farmer	13	315	1	None
Amor Eachus	Farmer	45	1,375	0?	None
Jonas Eyre	Farmer	90	5,500	12	200; 1799–
William Eyre	Farmer	162	2,565	3	None
Nicholas Fairlamb	?	?	?	?	600; 1806–1830
Robert Fairlamb	?	?	?	?	?
Robert Fairlamb, Jr.	Farmer	8	700	3	2,000; 1824–1829
William Gray	Physician	?	?	?	None
Robert Green	Farmer	200	3,635	10	None
William R. Hallowell	Potter	?	?	?	1,000; 1817–1826
Joshua Harrison	Farmer(?)	50	1,000	?	None
John Hibberd	Farmer	60	1,130	1	None
Thomas Horne	?	5	300	0	1,300; 1817–1820
John Hunt	Farmer-grazier	11	2,195	4	None
Halliday Jackson	Farmer	72	2,330	4	None
Abraham Johnson	Storekeeper	1	125	1	None
Charles Levis	?	?	?	?	350; 1822–1826
John Levis	Farmer	57	2,040	3	1,400; 1819–1835

Name	Occupation				
Asher Lobb	Farmer-cordwainer	60	1,475	1	None
Jeremiah McIlwain	?	?	?	?	10,000; 1822–
Abner Malin	Farmer	20	430	1	None
Gideon Malin	Farmer	17	760	3	None
Thomas Malin	Farmer	125	3,110	2	350; 1826–
George Miller	Farmer	130	2,800	7	1,250; 1823–1833
John Morgan, Sr.	Farmer	72	1,320	4	None
Aaron Oakford	Farmer	117	4,305	3	None
Isaac Oakford	Miller (fulling)	15	2,190	3	None
James Paist	Farmer	93	1,840	6	400; 1797–1811
John Pancoast	?	?	?	?	2,000; 1823–1832
Seth Pancoast	?	?	?	?	4,000; 1823–1833
John Pierce	Farmer	75	965	3	None
John Powell	Farmer	100	2,320	3	None
Joseph Powell	Farmer	69	1,280	4	None
Joseph Powell, Jr.	Farmer	117	1,770	3	None
Isaac Pyle	?	?	?	?	500; 1824–1828
John Rively	Shopkeeper	?	900	1	None
Obed Russell	Shopkeeper	10	270	0	None
John Serrill	Grazier	?	550	1	None
Isaac Sharpless	?	?	?	?	7,625; 1818–1828
William Shoemaker	?	?	?	?	500; 1799–1807
Isaac Smedley	Physician	50	800	1	None

HICKSITES (Continued)

Name	Occupation	Size of Property (in acres)	Total Value of Property (in $)	Number of Cattle	Mortgage (size in $ and years in effect)
James Smedley	Farmer	95	1,815	5	None
Thomas Steel	Grist miller	34	2,090	2	6,000?; 1815–1821
Joseph Taylor	Farmer	37	450	1	None
John W. Thatcher	Farmer	50	1,050	2	None
Joseph Thatcher	Farmer	133	5,005	3	None
Jonathan Thomas	Carpenter	7	400	1	1,600; 1814–1827
Seth Thomas	Farmer	65	1,810	4	None
Samuel West	Farmer	226	6,495	3	1,600; 1810–1811
Thomas West	Farmer	90	2,165	8	None
William West	Farmer	168	4,600	4	None
John Worrall	?	?	?	?	300; 1794–
Peter Worrall, Sr.	Farmer	62	2,075	3	None
John Yarnall	Farmer	38	1,130	5	None
William Yarnall (Middletown)	Farmer	80	2,135	3	None

F. Orthodox Quakers in Chester County

ORTHODOX

Name	Occupation	Size of Property (in acres)	Value of Property (in $)	Number of Cattle	Mortgage (size in $ and years in effect)
George G. Ashbridge	Farmer	100	6,715	9	None
Isaac Bailey	Farmer	100	2,055	3	1,000; 1819–1827
Thomas Bailey	Farmer(?)	?	Not property owner	3	None
William Bailey	Farmer	118	3,000	3	3,000; 1819–1828
John Baldwin	Farmer-miller	100	7,385	6	None
Jonathan Baldwin	Farmer	100	7,420	3	None
Samuel Baldwin	Farmer	115	5,420	6	None
Jacob Bennett	Farmer	229	9,900	6	None
John Bennington	Farmer	63	1,990	2	None
William Brown	Storekeeper	4	100	0	None
James Butler	Farmer	133	4,940	4	None
Caleb Chalfante, Jr.	Farmer	80	3,840	2	None
Benjamin Cope	Farmer	97	4,910	5	None
Gerard Cope	Farmer	107	5,275	6	None

ORTHODOX (Continued)

Name	Occupation	Size of Property (in acres)	Value of Property (in $)	Number of Cattle	Mortgage (size in $ and years in effect)
Jonathan Cope	Farm and nonfarm	15	3,845	4	None
Samuel Cope	Farmer	114	5,800	6	None
Emanuel Darlington	Farmer	75	5,250	7	None
Job Darlington	Farmer	100	6,910	2	None
Benjamin Davis	Nonfarm	16	600	2	None
Emmor Davis	Farmer	130	4,900	2	None
John Davis	Miller	78	4,265	3	None
Charles Downing	Farmer	204	8,150	1	None
George A. Downing	Tanner	12	2,010	1	None
James Downing	Farmer	230	11,535	6	None
Thomas Downing	Farmer	200	6,590	4	None
Thomas Downing, Jr.	Farmer	135	4,320	3	None
John Edge	Farmer	100	5,400	5	None
Thomas Edge	Farmer	216	4,400	5	None
Enos Elderidge	Farmer	81	4,050	3	None
Joseph Elderidge	Farmer	107	3,805	3	None
Joseph Elderidge, Jr.	Miller	35	1,890	1	None
Edward Evans	Farmer	48	3,160	2	None
John Forsythe	Farmer	184	12,350	4	None

Davis Garrett	Farmer	147	8,105	9	660; 1820–1836
Robert Garrett	Farmer-miller	177	9,710	3	570; 1824–1827
James Gibbons (E. Bradford)	Farmer	160	2,940	11	1,200; 1811–1822
William Gibbons	Farmer	320	14,570	2	620; 1814–1826
Abner Griffith	Farmer	120	3,375	7	None
Ezra Haines	?	10	700	?	None
William Harry	Farmer	?	Not property owner	4	None
Abraham Hibbard	Farmer	67	3,700	14	None
Josiah Hibbard	Farmer	180	8,960	3	None
Curtis Hoopes	Farmer	207	14,470	2	None
Isaac G. Hoopes	Nonfarm	—	Not property owner	1	None
Samuel Hoopes	Nonfarm	—	1,210	1	None
Joseph Hunt	Farmer	82	1,835	3	None
Joshua Hunt	Farmer	126	4,600	8	2,000; 1823–1840
Nicholas Hurford	Farmer	90	2,690	2	None
Joseph W. Huset	Farmer	82	1,830	3	None
Jairus Hutchinson	Farmer	22	570	2	None
John James	Farmer	113	6,160	3	None
Samuel Jefferies	Nonfarm	—	5,430	0	2,500; 1826–1828
Samuel Jones	Farmer	270	12,975	5	None
Isaiah Kirk	Farmer	62	2,140	2	None

ORTHODOX (Continued)

Name	Occupation	Size of Property (in acres)	Value of Property (in $)	Number of Cattle	Mortgage (size in $ and years in effect)
David Lamborn	Farmer	33	1,560	2	None
Mordecai Larkin	Farmer-miller	100	4,499	7	None
John Lewis	Miller	44	3,305	3	1,350; 1819–1824
David Lightfoot	Farmer	141	4,055	7	2,500; 1816–1832
Jacob Lindley	?	?	?	?	1,000; 1823–1833
James Malin	Farmer	190	11,410	11	5,000; 1810–1827
John Malin	Farmer	150	8,870	3	None
Randal Malin	Farmer	127	6,120	10	None
George Maris	Farmer	94	2,590	3	None
Eli Matson	Farm and nonfarm	50	3,215	5	None
Isaiah Meredith	?	100	3,500	?	None
James Meredith	Farmer	40	1,470	2	None
Jesse Meredith	Nonfarm	—	1,215	1	1,100; 1824–1832
Enos Morris	Nonfarm	50	2,420	1	None
Abel Otley	Farmer(?)	65	2,625	0	None
Jonathan Parke	Farmer	75	4,600	4	None
Thomas A. Parke	Farmer	91	3,475	4	None
Pennock Passmore	Nonfarm	—	300	1	None

	Nonfarm	—	Not property owner		
Jacob Perdue				0	None
John Phillips	Farmer	65	4,060	4	None
John Phipps	Farmer	165	6,005	6	None
Jonathan Phipps	Farmer	180	5,910	5	None
Philip Price	Farmer	40	3,040	4	None
Isaac Pusey	Miller	75	5,830	2	None
William Pusey	Farmer	85	3,225	2	None
John Roberts	Farmer	232	15,360	4	None
Abner Rogers	Farmer	90	3,980	6	1,000; 1814–1845
Abraham Sharpless	Farmer	180	10,340	7	4,000; 1816–1823
Benjamin Sharpless	Farmer	122	6,480	4	None
Jesse Sharpless	Farmer	223	11,235	9	6,500; 1818–
Joshua B. Sharpless	Farmer	12	560	5	None
Lewis Sharpless	Farmer	150	6,740	5	None
Nathan Sharpless (Concordville)	Farmer	223	10,440	4	4,000; 1817–1818
Jeffrey Smedley	Farmer	101	6,150	4	None
Peter Smedley	Farmer	125	4,320	5	None
Peter Smedley, Jr.	Farm and nonfarm	38	1,670	2	None
Thomas Smedley	Farmer	80	4,085	6	None
Caleb Stroud	Miller	100	4,130	3	None
Samuel Swayne	Farmer	107	5,640	4	None
William Swayne	Farmer	182	5,255	3	None

ORTHODOX (Continued)

Name	Occupation	Size of Property (in acres)	Value of Property (in $)	Number of Cattle	Mortgage (size in $ and years in effect)
Isaac Taylor	Farmer	250	11,645	18	1,720; 1821–
Job Taylor	Farmer	116	3,725	7	3,200; 1823–1876
Eli Thomas	Farmer	112	4,775	5	None
Enos Thomas	Miller	90	5,225	2	None
Francis Thomas	Farmer	70	3,760	2	None
Isaac Thomas	Farmer	80	3,590	3	None
John R. Thomas	Farmer-miller	320	20,380	3	None
Richard Thomas	Farmer-miller	250	29,190	8	None
John W. Townshend	Nonfarm	–	6,800		None
John Trimble	Miller	45	3,710	1	None
Ezekiel White	Storekeeper	–	990		850; 1821–
Levi Wickersham	Farmer	45	1,990	6	None
Thomas Williamson	Nonfarm	–	265		None
Thomas Woodward	Farmer	154	9,480	4	600; 1822–1838
John Zoole	Farmer	?	Not property owner	2	None

G. Hicksite Quakers in Chester County

HICKSITES

Name	Occupation	Size of Property (in acres)	Value of Property (in $)	Number of Cattle	Mortgage (size in $ and years in effect)
William Allen (London Grove)	Farmer	110	5,350	2	None
James Bailey	Farmer	160	7,635	4	None
Joel Bailey	Farmer	80	3,490	1	800; 1802–1826
John Bailey	Farmer	188	8,445	6	None
Lewis Bailey	Farmer (renter)	95	Not property owner	2	None
Obed Bailey	Farmer	60	3,220	3	None
Reuben Bailey	Farmer	78	3,490	3	None
Aaron Baker	Farmer	134	2,863	2	None
George Barnard	Farmer	105	4,400	3	None
Jeremiah Barnard	Farmer	197	8,830	3	None
John Barnard	?	90	3,800	0?	2,000; 1815–1821; 4,000; 1826–1827
James Bennett	Farmer	63	3,720	3	1,200; 1798–1812

HICKSITES (Continued)

Name	Occupation	Size of Property (in acres)	Value of Property (in $)	Number of Cattle	Mortgage (size in $ and years in effect)
Thomas Bennett	Farmer	106	1,344	2	None
John Carlisle	Farmer	186	5,290	3	3,000; 1812–1826
David Carr	Farmer (and ?)	?	1,300	1	None
Caleb Chalfante	Farmer	105	3,880	5	None
Joshua Chambers	Farmer	105	3,977	1	None
John Chandler	Farmer(?)	½	175	1	None
Joseph Chandler	Farmer	68	2,760	2	None
Thomas Chandler	Farmer	94	2,880	2	None
William Chandler	Farmer	130	8,465	1	None
Isaac Cook	Miller	70	3,760	2	None
Ezra Cope	Farmer	54	3,840	5	2,000; 1813–1819; 4,100; 1825–1837
Thomas S. Cox	Tailor	–	–	?	None
Thomas Cox	Farmer(?)	33	1,875	0	None
William Cox	Farmer	104	3,410	6	None
William Cox, Jr.	Schoolmaster	–	–	?	None
Abraham Darlington (Thornbury)	Farmer	150	8,510	4	None
Amos Darlington	Farmer	109	11,735	3	None

	?	?	?	?	
George Darlington	?	?	?	?	6,300; 1823–1825
Amos Davis	Farmer	30	1,075	2	None
Joseph Davis, Sr.	Farmer	166	9,700	2	None
John Edwards	Farmer	68	2,365	1	None
Emmor Entriken	Farmer	70	3,800	5	None
Lewis Fell	Farmer	81	3,300	0	None
Abner Garrett	Farmer	150	7,285	9	None
Amos Garrett	Farmer	100	4,380	1	None
Benjamin Garrett	Miller	82	4,600	6	400; 1824–1835
George Garrett	Miller	150	7,805	3	1,400; 1818–1829
Isaac Garrett	Farmer	112	6,375	1	None
Joseph Garrett	Farmer	174	7,240	2	None
Levi Garrett, Jr.	Farmer and ?	37	1,740	1	None
Nathan Garrett	Farmer	190	8,610	3	1,000; ?–1830
William Garrett	Farmer	110	5,390	11	None
William Garrett, Jr.	Miller	19	2,150	0	None
Joseph Guest	Farmer	95	2,680	4	None
David Haines	Nonfarm	–	810	1	150; 1826–1830
George Haines	Farmer (and ?)	30	2,265	3	None
Moris Hall	Farmer (renter)	100	Not property owner	1	None
Simon Hawley	Nonfarm	–	Not property owner	1	None
Job Hayes	Farmer	160	5,390	8	None

HICKSITES (Continued)

Name	Occupation	Size of Property (in acres)	Value of Property (in $)	Number of Cattle	Mortgage (size in $ and years in effect)
William Hibberd	Farmer(?)-tanner(?)	37	1,730	8	None
Abner Hoopes	?	30	2,250	0	530; 1821–1832
Caleb Hoopes	Farmer	94	6,065	8	3,000; 1825–1835
Enos Hoopes	Farmer	94	2,418	3	None
Henry Hoopes	Nonfarm	—	500	0	None
John Hoopes	Nonfarm	—	200	0	225; 1809–1845
Marshall Hoopes	Farmer	90	5,835	5	1,500; 1826–1835
William Huey	Farmer	235	13,470	5	5,000; 1814–1825
Joseph Hughs	Farmer	125	3,830	2	None
Thomas Jacobs	Farmer (renter)	250	Not property owner	1	None
Taylor Jeffries	Farmer	127	6,525	8	None
Mordecai Lee	Nonfarm	12	1,090	1	None
Elijah Lewis	Farmer	83	6,205	20	4,080; 1817–
John O. Lewis	?	2	Not property owner	1	None
Caleb Maris	Miller	118	5,730	7	None
John W. Marshall, Jr.	Farmer	146	4,230	3	170; 1813–1816

John Meredith	?	69	1,242	0?	450; 1817–1827
Isaac Miller	Farmer	150	7,020	10	None
Isaac Moore	Farmer	80	3,070	3	None
James Painter	Farmer	150	6,805	6	None
George Passmore	Farmer	170	4,950	2	None
Thomas Passmore	Farmer	100	4,075	2	None
John Patchell	Farmer	107	3,585	2	1,700; 1827–1835
Abraham Pennock	Farmer	200	11,275	3	None
James Pennock	Farmer	100	4,785	2	None
James Pennock, Jr.	Farmer	25	600	1	None
John Pennock	Miller	½	1,000	1	1,720; 1813–1819?
Joseph Pennock	Farmer	60	3,290	5	965; 1816–
Moses Pennock	?	?	?	?	4,000; 1818–1833
Thomas Pennock	Miller	28	1,635	2	None
Jeremiah Pratt	Farmer	50	2,730	2	None
Roberts Pratt	Farmer	210	9,865	9	None
Benjamin Price	Farmer	140	6,760	5	500; 1814–1820
Abner Pusey	Farmer-tanner	120	6,000	5	None
Benjamin Pusey	?	?	?	?	4,000; 1816–1822
David Pusey	Farmer	120	4,565	7	None
Enoch Pusey	?	?	?	?	800; 1803–1814
James Pusey	Miller	54	2,610	2	None
John Pusey	Farmer	52	1,780	3	None
Reuben Pusey	Tanner	25	1,770	1	None

HICKSITES (Continued)

Name	Occupation	Size of Property (in acres)	Value of Property (in $)	Number of Cattle	Mortgage (size in $ and years in effect)
Solomon Pusey	Farmer	95	2,400	4	None
Stephen Pusey	Nonfarm	–	Not property owner	?	None
Isaac Pyle	Miller	212	18,145	2	None
Robert Pyle	Farmer	65	2,820	2	400; 1820–1827
Samuel Pyle	Farmer	40	940	3	650; 1802–1809
Thomas Pyle	Farmer	90	4,610	1	None
Thomas Pyle, Jr.	Farmer	37	1,552	1	None
Joseph Roberts	Nonfarm	15	2,500	2	530; 1806–1824
Benjamin Rogers	Nonfarm	8	475	1	(?) 1801–1812
John Sharpless	Farmer	158	8,445	10	14,000; 1810–1819?
William Sharpless	Farmer(renter)	150	Not property owner	2	None
Isaac Smedley	Nonfarm	69	1,505	2	2,000; 1808–1809
Benjamin and Caleb Swayne (co-owners)	Tanners	92	6,060	9	3,000; 1826–1840
Caleb Swayne, Jr.	Farmer	65	2,375	2	None
Joseph L. Taylor	Farmer	112	7,025	3	400; 1824–1828
Lownes Taylor	Miller	68	7,725	3	None

Name	Occupation				
William Taylor (Westtown)	Farmer	10	650	1	650; 1815–1819
Mordecai Thomas	Farmer-miller	115	7,180	10	None
William Thomas	Miller	15	2,630	6	None
David Walton	Farmer	92	4,975	1	None
Joshua Walton	Farmer	75	2,955	2	None
Benjamin Webb	?	?	?	?	1,000; 1812–1824
Ezekiel Webb	Miller	94	2,750	1	None
(E. Marlborough) Thomas Webb	Farmer-miller	156	5,385	4	3,000; 1824–1845
Reuben White	Farmer	50	1,955	1	None
Ellis Williams	Farmer	144	7,095	12	None
Ephraim Wilson	Farmer	149	5,740	2	None
George Wilson	Farmer	35	1,190	3	None
Joshua Woodward	Farmer	22	690	1	None
James Woolaston	?	?	?	?	1,790; 1816–1830
Jesse Yarnall	Farmer	40	2,645	4	None
Walker Yarnall	Farmer	160	9,825	2	None

Bibliographical Essay

The sources on which this book is based can be followed in the footnotes. No purpose would be served by reviewing those sources here. However, it does seem useful briefly to review other treatments of the Hicksite Separation and relevant studies in the sociology of religion.

There are many general histories of Quakerism which touch on the Separation and its causes. Despite a tendency toward partisanship, most of these histories are balanced and are still of interest to the modern student. Of the nineteenth century works the most useful are Alan and Richard Thomas, *A History of the Society of Friends* (Philadelphia, 1895); Samuel M. Janney, *The History of the Society of Friends from its Rise to the Year 1828*, IV (Philadelphia, 1867); and William Hodgson, *The Society of Friends in the Nineteenth Century*, I (Philadelphia, 1875). Elbert Russell's *The History of Quakerism* (New York, 1942) and Rufus Jones's *The Later Period of Quakerism*, 2 vols. (New York, 1921), are both important but at times seem based more on intuition than research. Perhaps the most striking characteristic of all these works is their tendency to repeat one another and to echo arguments initially framed by participants in the schism.

Recent studies have attained a high level of scholarship. Howard Brinton's *Friends for Three Hundred Years* (New York, 1952) is an excellent intellectual history of the Quakers and provides interesting insights into the Separation. William Bacon Evans presents a reasoned statement of Orthodox sentiments in his *Jonathan Evans* (Boston, 1959). Bliss Forbush follows the career of Elias Hicks in a detailed biography *Elias Hicks: Quaker Liberal* (New York, 1956). It might, however, be argued that Forbush has exaggerated Hicks's "liberal" qualities.

Despite numerous treatments of the subject, a serious student of the Separation must still turn to statements made by participants. Unfortunately, there are few defenses of the Orthodox position. Some insights into Orthodoxy may be gained through Jeremiah Foster, *An Authentic Report*, 2 vols. (Philadelphia, 1831), in which appears testimony of Orthodox and Hicksite leaders as to the causes of the Separation. Generally though, Orthodox rationale must be pieced together from fragmentary sources.

Hicksites left many revealing accounts of their views. The best place to begin is *The Berean, A Religious Publication*, 4 vols. (Wilmington, Delaware, 1824–1828). Similarly important is Benjamin Ferris and Eliphalet Gilbert, *The Letters of Paul and Amicus* (Philadelphia, 1823). These theological discussions should be supplemented with more subjective personal descriptions of the Separation. Of these, the manuscripts of Halliday Jackson and Benjamin Ferris in the Friends Historical Library are especially helpful. Also important are the Journals of Elias Hicks (New York, 1832); John Comly (Philadelphia, 1853); Edward Hicks (Philadelphia, 1851) and Jesse Kersey (Philadelphia, 1851). John Cockburn, *Cockburn's Review* (Philadelphia, 1829) contains many of the Separation's important documents.

J. Milton Yinger's *Religion, Society and the Individual* (New York, 1957) is an excellent introduction to the sociology of religion. Yinger's clear presentation of theoretical material is well supplemented by the empirical articles which appear in the latter half of the book. Elizabeth K. Nottingham's *Re-*

ligion and Society (New York, 1954); N. J. Demerath's *Social Class and American Protestantism* (Chicago, 1965); and W. S. Salisbury, *Religion in American Culture: A Sociological Interpretation* (Homewood, Illinois, 1964) add to Yinger's treatment of religion. Demerath's revisionist study is particularly important. Will Herberg's *Protestant, Catholic and Jew,* Anchor edition (New York, 1955) and H. Richard Niebuhr's *Social Sources of Denominationalism* (New York, 1929) treat American religious history from a sociological viewpoint. Niebuhr qualifies his position in *The Kingdom of God in America,* Harper edition (New York, 1959). Further understanding of relationships between religion and socioeconomic change may be gained from Ernst Troeltsch, *The Social Teaching of the Christian Churches,* 2 vols., Torchbook edition (New York, 1960); Max Weber, *Protestant Ethic and the Spirit of Capitalism* (London, 1930); R. H. Tawney, *Religion and the Rise of Capitalism* (New York, 1926); Liston Pope, *Millhands and Preachers* (New Haven, Conn., 1942); Gerhard Lenski, *The Religious Factor,* revised edition (New York, 1963); W. W. Schroeder and V. Obenhaus, *Religion in American Culture* (New York, 1964); and Emery Battis, *Saints and Sectaries* (Chapel Hill, North Carolina, 1962).

Emile Durkheim's *Suicide* (New York, 1951) is a classic account of human responses to social change. This same theme is studied in Hans Toch, *The Social Psychology of Social Movements* (New York, 1965) and Hadley Cantril, *The Psychology of Social Movements* (New York, 1941). An inventory of recent social scientific findings appears in Bernard Berelson and Gary A. Steiner, *Human Behavior* (New York, 1964). No student of American society can ignore Robin Williams' *American Society: A Sociological Interpretation* (New York, 1960) and Robert K. Merton's closely and brilliantly argued *Social Theory and Social Structure,* revised edition (Glencoe, Illinois, 1957).

Index